Managing the Business for AS

Doug Waterson

Edited by: **Nancy Wall**

informe

Doug Waterson started his career in costing and accountancy before entering the teaching profession where he taught economics, business studies and accounts for 30 years, 25 of these as HOD at a successful East Yorkshire comprehensive. He is currently a principal examiner for Edexcel's 'A' level Business Studies course and also runs his own small accountancy business. Doug is a Fellow of the International Association of Book-keepers.

Nancy Wall was a teacher for the first half of her career. Since 1991 she has worked in curriculum development, with a particular interest in teaching strategies and classroom resource development. She is currently reviews editor of 'Teaching Business and Economics', the magazine of the Economics, Business and Enterprise Association. She has long experience of writing and editing resources for students.

© Anforme Ltd 2012
ISBN 978-1-905504-75-6
Anforme Ltd, Stocksfield Hall, Stocksfield, Northumberland NE43 7TN.
Typeset by George Wishart & Associates, Whitley Bay.
Printed by Potts Print (UK) Ltd.

Contents

Using this book

Most users of this book will be studying AS Business Studies, probably with a view to study at A2. This text covers Unit 2a, Managing the Business, and you will also be studying Unit 1, Developing New Business Ideas. Units 1 and 2a combined make up AS Business Studies. One of the aims of this book is to prepare a foundation for future work in this area.

Some of the chapters of this book provide background knowledge that will help you understand the key elements of Unit 2a. The introduction provides a snapshot of business in the UK and examines, briefly, why people go into business. Most chapters follow the specification of the course and cover the four areas of unit content as set out by Edexcel. Just occasionally, the order of the topics is changed slightly to make the content easier to understand.

To give the reader a rounded view of how businesses operate, there is some repetition of concepts from Unit 1 together with some additional background information. Using your prior knowledge is important in this subject, and repeated use of key ideas should make studying easier and enhance your understanding.

The text uses examples and situations from real businesses, ranging from sole traders, where the owner has few or no employees, to the largest of multi-national companies. In between you will find examples from small and large businesses in the primary, secondary and tertiary sectors. You will come across the increasing influence of the latest technologies; examples will reflect the move towards business via the internet and away from city and town centres.

You should try to use the examples provided to help you to understand the course and to motivate you to discover examples of your own, both in your local environment and nationally. There is so much information available to you but a cautionary note should be added. Don't believe or trust everything you read. Try and verify information; discuss it with your teachers and use it as a basis for discussion.

The book has not set out to replicate specific examination questions, although many questions are framed as you would find them in the examination room. The Edexcel website provides past papers along with detailed mark schemes. Also Edexcel asks principal examiners to compile a Results Plus report which looks at student answers and offers comments as to how marks are achieved, or indeed lost. When the time comes to practice exam technique, be sure to get access to these sources.

This text seeks to provide further stimulus by offering opportunities to test your understanding and to discuss relevant issues. These opportunities are to be found in the real business case studies, the special tips, and the 'show what you know' questions. With the many clear and concise definitions, it is hoped that you will enjoy enhancing your knowledge of the subject matter and be well prepared, not only for examination success but also for entry into the business world.

Introduction

Setting the scene

In July 2011 Colin and Chris Wear won over £161m on the Euro Lottery, instantly becoming one of Britain's richest couples. Their wealth puts them on a par with David and Victoria Beckham. Unfortunately for most people trying to make their way in life and in business the journey is longer and harder.

Business Population Estimates were published by the Department for Business, Innovation and Skills (BIS) in May 2011. They show that there are 4.5m UK private sector enterprises (employing 22.5m people), of which sole traders comprise 65%, companies 25% and partnerships around 10%. Small and medium sized businesses (SMEs), those with fewer than 250 employees, account for 99.9% of all private sector enterprises.

As a comparison, government figures showed that at the end of the first quarter of 2011, 6.15m people were employed in the public sector. The unemployment rate for the three months to September 2011 was 8.3% of the economically active population, a total of 2.62m people.

These figures show that nearly 80% of people in employment work in the private sector. (Only about 2% work in the voluntary sector, in charities or not-for-profit organisations.) Many of these businesses will be 'one man bands'; many others will have fewer than 5 employees. In 2010 there was an increase of 48,000 in business start ups, coupled with a falling business failure rate but the failure rate, i.e. businesses dying, was still higher than the birth rate, i.e. businesses starting. In the UK one in three new businesses fail in the first three years. Put more positively, two out of three survive the first three years.

It is in the interest of the government of the day that business start ups increase, that existing businesses do well and that they grow. Without a thriving private sector, the government wouldn't receive much of the tax revenue which enables it to maintain its public works programmes, such as building schools and hospitals. It wouldn't be able to support local authorities and it wouldn't be able to provide the funds for our armed forces.

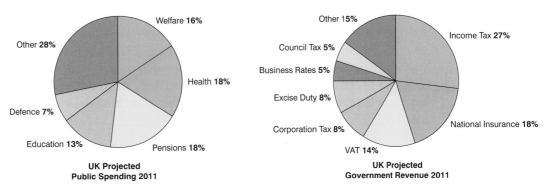

UK Projected Public Spending 2011 — UK Projected Government Revenue 2011

Source: The Treasury

An examination of projected government revenue for 2011 shows 45 per cent of that revenue coming from income tax and national insurance which is paid by people in employment. Given that 80 per cent of those in employment work in the private sector, most of that money must come from those employed by private sector businesses. These businesses then contribute a further 8 per cent of revenue through Corporation Tax and collect most of the 14 per cent VAT on behalf of the government. Business Rates contribute a further 5 per cent and excise duties such as tax levies on alcohol and tobacco, which are collected by private businesses, contribute a further 8 per cent. Even within the 15 per cent for 'other' we will find vehicle excise duty to which private businesses and their employees make a significant contribution.

It should be clear that the government is better able to function properly when the economy is doing well, and less able to do so when growth in the economy is sluggish. It is in the government's best interests to provide an economic environment that allows businesses to set up easily and provides both support to fledgling businesses and encouragement to existing ones.

Why go into business?

There are many reasons why people go into business and this question is considered in more detail later. But those who choose to do so have a range of significant characteristics. Adam Smith, in his 1776 publication 'Wealth of Nations' first coined the phrase 'a nation of shopkeepers', and the term was used disparagingly by Napoleon when he mocked England's preparedness for war. The phrase is still used, possibly because, in the 20th century, men returning from the two great wars found jobs hard to come by, partly because women were carrying out many of the jobs previously done by men. So they opened shops and other small businesses. Many of these men had probably had enough of being given orders and decided to start out on their own – one of the main reasons why people start their own business today. Those who use their initiative, work hard, are resilient, and are prepared to take risks are most likely to prosper. Together with creativity and self-confidence, these characteristics provide a framework for success in business.

Whether people go into business for profit or for non-profit motives (such as creating an ethical organisation), there is never a shortage of potential entrepreneurs. It is possible that with the wave of redundancies in 2011, many of them in the public sector, we will see new budding entrepreneurs, fuelled by redundancy payments, seeking to make their way as the next James Dyson, Richard Branson or George Davies.

What is the difference between theory and practice?

Before writing this text, I taught economics and business studies for 30 years and prior to that worked in industry. For the past six years I have run my own accountancy business, so have some experience in this area. Undoubtedly the biggest difference between theory and practice is seen when the comfort blanket of theory is replaced by the cold wind of reality. There is no amount of theory that can replicate being in business for real. There are, however, a number of advantages in having prior knowledge of what to expect – the need to plan carefully, to prepare properly, the types of documents needed. These undoubtedly help provide a stepping-stone into the business world.

Fortunately students of business studies do not have to deal with HMRC (Her Majesty's Revenue & Customs). The number of departments and offices in that huge organisation can make progress slow. All new businesses have to register with HMRC and when their turnover rises above the VAT threshold (£73,000 per year in 2011) they have to register for VAT (value added tax) as well. All businesses have to fill in forms, usually online. Self Assessment is a requirement for the millions of sole traders and if you don't do it yourself you have to pay an accountant to do it for you. Paperwork abounds and records must be kept. This comes as a shock to many of the self-employed who would really like to concentrate on what they know and do best. Budding entrepreneurs should be aware of this. When businesses fail, poor procedure is as likely a cause as poor forecasting.

Jane Stobie obtained a degree in nutritional studies after she realised that she wanted her career to be in food and catering. She worked in the NHS for six years and for Anglia Crown (which provides readymeals for hospitals) for two years. There she had the idea for Kealth Foods, providing meals for sufferers of dysphagia, who find it difficult to swallow. The business took two years to get off the ground and Jane had to borrow £60,000 from her mother in law. The NHS was a big customer and things were going well until she took on a mentor who tried to encourage her to expand her specialist food business too quickly. Fortunately she spotted the danger and the business survived and prospered. Today it employs 50 people and has a turnover of over £5m since she created her own brand of baby food.

Her advice for people considering founding their own company is "make sure you have enough money." She added that they shouldn't let her bad experience with a mentor put others off turning to more experienced business people for advice. "Do your research, and talk to other business owners. Seek as much advice as possible to ensure you understand the pitfalls."

Good fish and chips

I used to take students out of school to look at businesses in a particular area, to see if they could identify potential business opportunities. Before we did this we would work with them on ways of conducting market research. We would ask them what type of business they thought was lacking in the area and they would answer immediately, maybe a hairdressers, a fast food outlet or a greengrocers. Then we asked the students to consider why such an outlet was not in place already. Only then did most stop to think that it might be because there was not enough demand to be satisfied at a profit.

Some of my students had to investigate potential business opportunities in some detail. One of them, Jack, decided that a fish and chip shop could be opened successfully in a particular location. I advised him to look at the past history of a nearby shop where two previous 'chippies' had opened and then closed in a relatively short period of time. Nevertheless he went ahead and based his study on this idea, carrying out as much market research as you could reasonably expect from a 17 year old. His project was thorough and it received a good grade.

Imagine my surprise when 4 or 5 years later I walked into this shop and found Jack not only working there, but personally running the business and doing well. When I asked what made his shop different from the previous outlets he told me that there was always a potential market as there were a lot of houses close by; that the previous owners were opening at the wrong hours and that he gave better customer service – including free delivery locally. Evening opening hours had previously been 7pm to 11pm, hoping to catch the pub trade. Now they were 4pm to 8pm, to catch people coming home from work, too busy or too tired to cook.

Questions

1. In your judgement, which factors were most important in leading to the success of Jack's business? Explain your thinking.

2. Could there have been other significant factors, not mentioned above? Give as many possible examples as you can. (You could explain what 'better customer service' might mean in this context.)

Marketing

Marketing is the management process involved in identifying, anticipating, and satisfying consumer requirements profitably. Some observers might argue that this immediately presents a conflict of interest between the needs of consumers, who want products to be as cheap as possible, and businesses that want to make as much profit as possible. This need not be the case, for a number of reasons. First of all many consumers are looking for quality rather than low prices – why would there be such a range of clothes outlets if this were not so? Secondly, even those who are price conscious can be satisfied at a profit if costs can be minimised and volumes maximised. Somewhere in between the two, other businesses will do well with their own **unique selling points** (USPs) and ways of offering value for money. Clearly, Jack was offering a good value meal at a price that attracted the customers.

> **Unique selling points** (USPs) are particular features of the product or service that a business offers its customers, characteristics that set it apart from competitors.

Market research

Marketing objectives

Marketing objectives are the goals that a business is trying to achieve through its marketing. They could relate to profit or sales revenue or both. For example, many small businesses in the start-up phase will find a niche market where they can compete successfully with established businesses. Even so, they must make a profit to survive and must sell enough to cover costs. As they become established they may see expanding output as their primary objective, perhaps aiming at an eventual mass market. This will require very different strategies, perhaps including lower prices. Good decisions in both situations require the best possible market research.

At every stage of development, the business will have targets for sales revenue. Marketing objectives relate to the decisions that must be made as to prices, product design and advertising. Examples include increasing sales, raising brand awareness, enhancing brand or corporate image and promoting brand loyalty.

Market research

Advertising and soaps

Many readers will know that Coronation Street has been shown on ITV in the UK for over 50 years. The 'soap' is considered to be prime time television and as such, because of its large audiences, which in the early days of commercial television would often exceed 20 million, commanded top prices for advertisements. In those days cigarette advertising was frequently seen on commercial channels and an advert for Strand cigarettes was shown in the programme's commercial break. It featured a man in a long raincoat with the collar turned up, standing under a viaduct that looked similar to one in the programme. The advert had a strap line – 'you're never alone with a Strand'. Advertisers who paid mega money for prime time slots expected to see large increases in sales. This campaign failed. Follow-up research found out that smokers perceived the 'man in the mac' to be lonely and they didn't want to be seen in the same way.

Questions

1. Why is market research important?
2. What kinds of market research might have prevented the above situation? Be as precise as you can.

Market research can be quantitative or qualitative. (Go back to your work on Unit 1 if you need to clarify this.) It involves collecting, collating and analysing data to be used in the marketing of goods and services. This information is designed to help entrepreneurs make better business decisions. Good market research may show what ideas not to pursue but even marketing agencies can get it wrong sometimes. Still, better research might have stopped the Coronation Street advert from being a flop.

A key factor for many potential businesses may be the market size and in particular, whether the market is growing or not. In a time of recession many markets will be shrinking. But this does not mean that all businesses face a declining market. Some people may be buying fish and chips from Jack instead of going out for a meal. Brighton did well in the summers of 2009 and 2010 because many people went there for a day out when they had to forego expensive holidays during the recession. This means that careful thought has to be given to market positioning.

In general, all businesses need to be **market oriented**. They can increase both sales and profits when they study customer requirements and adapt when these change – as they frequently do. Strategic planning has to take account of both consumer preferences and competition from other businesses. Market research is therefore a key element in successful business planning.

Market orientation applies to the business that will focus on customer needs before deciding on product design, price and promotion.

All businesses need to identify a target market. Where markets are segmented, maybe by location or consumer preferences, businesses will be able to find specific niches where their products can compete successfully. Pricing, quality, attractiveness and value for money will be crucial. Planning the details creates a need for the best possible information.

For many bigger businesses, those with mass markets, increasing market share is an important goal. This may mean planning a range of carefully positioned products so that they can access as many different market segments as possible.

Examining the data

Secondary research

Market research can be broken down into two types: desk or secondary research and field or primary research. Much secondary data is available on the internet but caution must be advised: not all sites can be trusted. Some useful secondary information is made available by the government, through census surveys, economic reports and business advice.

Some information can be gained from competitors, without doing anything underhand. Published accounts, product ranges and web site information are readily available. Publications that are trade specific, e.g. *The Grocer* can be helpful. *Marketing* magazine carries interesting data and their web site has good advertising stories. Of course one of the most informative sources of secondary data for any ongoing business will be their own sales figures, both budgeted and actual, and a breakdown of costs.

Qualitative research

Primary research

Primary or field research can be obtained in a number of ways, depending on the product and who it is to be used by. However, if the information gathered is to be useful the questions asked must produce meaningful answers that are relevant and appropriate. Larger businesses will use trained field researchers to undertake qualitative research. Focus groups – small groups that can discuss their tastes and attitudes with a researcher – can provide good qualitative research findings. Smaller businesses can usually keep in direct touch with their customers more easily. Customers like to feel valued and asking potential and previous customers for their views may help to achieve brand loyalty if those people feel their views are being considered.

A new nursery

When setting up a children's nursery in South Cave, East Yorkshire, Matt and Janina Simpson had to identify market trends. The village of South Cave had close road links to Hull and to the motorway that fed Leeds. Through looking at figures available from the local council they could see that the numbers of houses in the area was increasing and that demand for family houses was driving that increase. There was already one nursery but that was full.

The Simpsons were fortunate to find premises at the local community and sports hall, for which Matt had helped to raise funds. An added bonus was that the premises were next to the local primary school so parents with two young children (one of school age and one under that age) could bring them both at the same time. From readily available publicity material they could see what the market rates for fees were. OFSTED published detailed guides as to what their premises should have, what qualifications their staff should acquire and what procedures to follow. Their product was child care and as both were practising teachers they had a good knowledge of teaching methods. Their nursery manager had experience in the field. Primary research was carried out by word of mouth, by delivery of flyers in the local area and by making use of village fetes to promote their services.

Three months after deciding to take the plunge they had all policies in place and premises ready, and two months later they were ready to start, with 8 children enrolled. Within 3 months this number had doubled and their breakeven point had been exceeded.

(questions overleaf)

Questions

1. Why might a study of the type of houses in an area be worthwhile for any business wishing to set up in the local community?

2. Briefly explain, in context, two types of secondary market research and two methods of primary market research that Matt and Janina would have used.

Market research informs the decisions that businesses must take and helps to reduce risks. Research carried out at an early stage may prevent the waste of resources involved in developing and launching a product that fails. Without market research, especially primary research, businesses will find it difficult to understand the needs of their potential customers. Market research can identify trends and help businesses to adapt to changing market conditions.

Market research does not guarantee success. Indeed something like 90 per cent of all products fail, at some stage. Sometimes failure is due to poor research but even with extensive and systematic research, some products fail to sell well. However some products have international appeal, and even quite small businesses can sometimes increase their market size using the internet.

Show what you know

Consider the following firms and products and decide whether they might be regarded as failures, giving reasons for your conclusions:

- Was Woolworth's a failure? After all they were in existence for over 100 years; most of those years were highly successful for the company. But Woolworth's were the leading music retailer in the 1960s and perhaps their market research didn't spot the changes in how customers liked to access their music. Perhaps Zavvi was a victim of the same failure to spot trends and not adapt to them?

- Was Polaroid a success or a failure? (With a Polaroid camera, you could take the picture and within a minute, the print came out of a slot on the camera. The company closed in 2008 after 60 years of production, defeated by the competition from digital cameras.)

Mass markets

Niche or mass marketing?

The vast majority of businesses start off small and many stay that way. Very few owners can afford to target a mass market as a business objective. Some highly specialised producers thrive as small or medium sized enterprises. Those that do target growth have to have enough cash to pay for expanded marketing operations. Inevitably, achieving growth may take time and a substantial investment.

The new nursery described above would always be a small business, although the Simpsons might decide to expand by opening nurseries in different locations. Even so it is likely to be in a niche market because nurseries need to be conveniently located and there would be few cost savings associated with being part of a larger organisation. In contrast, Dyson, in the case study on page 8, hoped for a mass market for its innovative vacuum cleaners right from the start.

In between, the vast majority of businesses start small but expand as soon as they can see that their market has growth potential. Tesco (page 7) provides a striking example. Many businesses grow up to a certain point, at which their size is appropriate to the product and the market. From then on they do not seek spectacular growth and may choose to follow other paths, for example maintaining sales and market share. T.J.Hughes might have been like this (see page 8).

Using bigger, technically advanced machines can gain economies of scale.

Mass markets

Tesco

It is unlikely that Jack Cohen, the founder of Tesco, the leading British supermarket, thought much about global domination when he set out to sell surplus groceries from a stall in London in 1919, yet he expanded quickly, floating the company on the London Stock Exchange in 1947. Tesco's growth was a mixture of organic growth and acquisition. (Organic growth means that the business expands from within, i.e. by creating more and bigger supermarkets. Acquisition means taking over or merging with other companies, so gaining control of their supermarkets without having to set them up.) With both, the company steadily increased sales, revenue, profit and market share.

Tesco appears to have gained its USP by appealing to all segments of the market and marketing has probably played a key part in this, enabling the firm to get a competitive advantage over its rivals.

Questions

1. Explain why Tesco might be described as successful, giving as many reasons as you can.
2. List all the examples you can of Tesco's measures to retain customers and increase sales revenue.

Economies of scale

A key factor in business decisions about growth is whether there are potential **economies of scale**. These exist when expanding output leads to falling costs per unit. Sometimes there are technical reasons for this – using bigger and more technically advanced machines in manufacturing may cuts costs dramatically. So the most competitive producer may also be the biggest. Falling costs make it easy to create a mass market because prices can be cut, bringing products within reach for people who previously could not afford them.

Economies of scale can also be very important in marketing. You can see that expensive TV adverts may be just the way to create a mass market, but the business has to be big enough to afford them. This cuts both ways: if a mass market can be created, the advertising costs could be small in comparison to the extra sales revenue achieved.

> **Economies of scale** occur when increasing output leads to lower costs per unit. These may include production costs and marketing costs. There can be financial economies too, as bigger firms are better able to access cheap finance.

Maintaining sales and market share

T.J. Hughes, a large retailer of discounted fashion and household brands, was forced to close in 2011. It had tried to expand by buying Woolworth's branches but then faced dramatic falls in revenue and profit, probably because of the UK recession. Maintaining sales and market share might not seem to be an ambitious objective for a successful business, but in a recession, many firms would settle for just that. It may be that in the future T.J.Hughes will survive in some form, but probably operating on a much smaller scale.

In some very competitive markets, medium-sized and small enterprises can survive quite well alongside very big companies. The construction industry is like this – many plumbers are sole traders with no employees at all, doing everything themselves. Small local building companies will build the odd house for someone who has a bit of land, or do repairs and extensions. While Balfour Beatty builds motorways, bridges and airports with a turnover of £10 billion a year, and Wates and Bovis make just under £1 billion a year with their housing estates and other projects.

Market share

Businesses can be highly successful without growing ever larger. Their marketing objectives will reflect their overall business objectives and the trading environment in which they operate. Very often, if personal services are involved, small scale businesses have much to offer. There are still many single salons in hairdressing, doing quite well, yet even there chains have emerged, like Toni and Guy with their 400 salons.

Product differentiation

When a business wants to carve out a market for itself, it will always try to create a product that stands out from the rest. Sometimes it will be a USP; equally there may be scope for developing a completely new product, like the iPad. Retailers go out of their way to distinguish themselves from the competition, as you would have seen when thinking about Tesco. Key product features may be significant in terms of the performance of the product – Miele household goods are well known for their reliability. Or they may be about customer perceptions – as with fashion items. Clever product differentiation may be a marketing objective in itself – as it clearly is for Apple.

> **Product differentiation** means making a product distinctive in some way, so that customers will choose it in preference to competing products. It can apply to services just as much as to manufactured products.

Marketing objectives

The bagless vacuum cleaner

James Dyson has established a strong presence on the vacuum cleaner market by inventing a bagless vacuum cleaner. Now he has used his high-tech approach to invent a bladeless fan, aiming his product at a niche market willing to pay high prices for an innovative product. Dyson has combined product differentiation with new product development and innovation, marketing objectives which have the power to create completely new markets.

Questions

1. Describe Dyson's marketing objectives.

2. To what extent would the success of the Dyson cleaner have been the result of the marketing effort?

3. Mobile phone manufacturers and operators are constantly changing the boundaries of what we can do with technology. Select one business and consider its marketing objectives. How has it achieved success?

James Dyson faced a daunting challenge. He was looking to compete with a generic brand – Hoover. So dominant was Hoover in the market for vacuum cleaners, that people often called their vacuum cleaner a hoover. (The same thing happened with tissues and Kleenex.) Dyson has become the market leader in vacuum cleaner sales.

Niches and competition

Niche markets

Many people in business want to make a living but are not interested in becoming a business icon like Richard Branson or James Dyson. They may be very happy catering for a niche market. Niche markets are often a little less competitive than mass markets. Businesses that cater for mass markets may not find it profitable to aim their marketing at small, rather individualistic niche markets. That said, new technologies are making short production runs cheaper, so some big companies are now looking at niche markets. Nevertheless, niche markets offer frequent opportunities for imaginative product differentiation.

With slightly less competition, businesses in niche markets may be able to charge higher prices. They can concentrate on the specific needs of customers in their niche. A delicatessen located near to a giant supermarket may be able to compete on the quality and variety of its stock, even though the supermarket will be competing on price. Convenience stores, whose niche is the group of people living nearby, will almost always charge significantly more than the supermarket. They have to because they cannot buy in bulk, so costs are higher. But if customers value convenience, they will survive.

Some niche markets arise from special personal interests. Model railway enthusiasts may buy their treasures from internet suppliers who can sell across a huge area. They can keep overheads low because they do not need a High Street retail outlet with high rent, and can access a large enough market to make a living. However, many people think they can make a living from a niche market, only to find that their costs are still greater than their sales revenue because the market is just not large enough to support them.

Many a business person has started out by identifying a business opportunity when they have failed to find a product or service themselves. This often works, but it requires very careful market research and marketing strategies that are closely linked to the specific circumstances.

Special tip
Students are correctly taught that marketing objectives should be SMART, an acronym that stands for specific, measured, agreed, realistic, and time specific. When using this in an examination situation, always try to put the message into the context of the chosen firm.

Chapter 2

The marketing mix

A successful marketing strategy will involve choosing a range of different approaches, which, together, will be capable of meeting the desired objectives. One way of looking at this process of decision making is to think about the **marketing mix**. This includes the **price** that customers must pay and the benefits that come from buying the product. These benefits will be the result of careful product design, based on a good understanding of the target market, and an accurate assessment of the price that people in this market will be willing and able to pay. You can see all this at work in the following case study.

Passenger lounges

Phil Cameron was a successful West End theatre producer but the highs and lows of the stage had sapped his energy. Cameron had had a globe-trotting childhood, even travelling alone from England to New Zealand at the age of 11. He decided to go into business on his own, applying to start an airline for business travellers. When he could not raise the funds he turned his attention to airport passenger lounges, places where he had spent many a long uncomfortable hour. He seized an opportunity to take over a lounge at New York's JFK airport and turned it into an executive lounge. He intended to provide facilities for first and business-class passengers. With a partner he raised £100,000, mainly from family and friends, opening The Lounge in January 2007. The venture made a substantial profit in the first 12 months and, with further capital from private investors he opened another lounge at Gatwick and two at Stansted. Travellers pay £15 to £20 to spend up to 3 hours inside.

Source: Adapted from 'How I made it.' – *Sunday Times*, 6 March 2011

Questions

1. How would Phil Cameron have worked out what to charge and how to run his lounges?
2. Could he have charged more than £20 for a 3-hour visit?

Marketing mix

Product benefits can be enhanced in various ways; the effect will be to make the product better value for money. But sales are not increased only by price or product changes. **Promotion** of the product through advertising, packaging, special offers and the provision of information can be very important. This may create a favourable image for the product, or it may simply inform potential customers of its existence.

Distribution can also play a part in the marketing process. This can influence the way products are made available to potential customers. By carefully selecting the retail outlets they will use, businesses seek to make their products easily accessible to as many people as possible. So when doing their market research, they may look for locations which will be most likely to bring in the customers. Footfalls (the typical number of people walking by) may have to be balanced against the rental costs of the outlet. Discounts may be needed to persuade independent stockists to sell the product. Businesses even get involved in the way the retail outlet displays their products. Or they may try to 'cut out the middleman' by selling direct to customers rather than using a wholesaler as an intermediary. This aspect of marketing is often referred to as '**place**'.

> The **marketing mix** includes decisions relating to **price**, **product**, **promotion** and **place**, sometimes referred to as the 4 Ps.

The best possible marketing mix will be the one that has been precisely matched to the needs of the situation. (See Figure 1.) Any one of the 4Ps can be crucial in determining the outcome in terms of quantity sold, sales revenue or profit. Business success depends on selecting marketing strategies that are appropriate for the product and the market. That means deciding which aspects of the 4Ps are most important and developing them.

Figure 1: Developing the marketing mix

Using the marketing mix

It's an ill wind that blows nobody any good

The consumer appliance industry suffered a sharp downturn during 2010 and 2011 but Dyson appeared to buck the trend.

Energy shortages after the Japanese tsunami pushed up sales of Dyson's bladeless fan by 250 per cent as people switched off air conditioning to reduce the strain on the power grid. Sales in America grew 40 per cent in 2010 and the company's market share in Britain breached 30 per cent, compared to 22 per cent in 2009.

The company introduced a cordless vacuum cleaner in 2010 and it promptly sold out. Total sales increased from £770m in 2009 to £887m in 2010, while profits were up 9 per cent at £206m, helped by innovations such as the Airblade hand dryer. Dyson invested £45m in research and development (R&D) in 2010.

Although Dyson operates in 52 markets it has yet to venture into China, India or Brazil. Sir James explained this by claiming that the upper middle classes in these countries did not use vacuum cleaners themselves as they often had servants. He added that the company's growth (they are the biggest firm in the UK vacuum cleaner market, by some margin) flew in the face of poor results from competitors Electrolux and Whirlpool. He was critical of Vax (another rival) which sells the Hoover range, accusing them of patent infringement.

Dyson employed 200 new engineers in Britain in 2010, doubling the number of highly skilled workers at its site. They plan to bring that number up to 700. However, Sir James said his company was struggling to find a sufficient number of workers, particularly graduates willing to join the business, despite a starting salary of £25,200 and a joining bonus of £3,000. He said that demand for engineers would quadruple over the coming years with the number of positions already outstripping the number of people graduating with relevant degrees.

Questions

1. Explain one reason why Dyson should regularly update the marketing mix for his bladeless fan.

(4 marks)

This 4 mark question would typically be awarded two marks for knowledge, one mark for application and one mark for analysis.

(continued overleaf)

2. Explain why Sir James Dyson would be keen to protect the originality of his inventions through patenting them. (If you aren't sure about patents, see pages 19-20.) (6 marks)
   This 6 mark question would typically be awarded 2 marks for knowledge, two marks for application and two marks for analysis.

3. Identify which areas of the marketing mix Dyson would need to concentrate on as it seeks to maintain and increase its share of the vacuum cleaner market. (8 marks)
   This 8 mark question would typically be awarded two marks for knowledge, two marks for application, two marks for analysis and 2 marks for evaluation.

4. Almost half of the world's population live in China, India and Brazil. Evaluate the need for a mass marketing strategy as opposed to a niche marketing strategy, if Dyson was to attempt to sell its consumer products in these countries. (14 marks)
   This 14 mark question would typically be awarded three marks for knowledge, three marks for application, three marks for analysis and five marks for evaluation.

The business that starts out by identifying a gap in the market will design its product precisely to fit the gap – as Phil Cameron (page 10) did with his passenger lounge, which catered for people who did not have an airline-provided lounge. He positioned his product carefully in the market. But of course markets never stand still. Very few businesses can afford to stay with the existing marketing mix for long: they must adapt to market change. Dyson faced falling demand for its vacuum cleaners as the recession developed. Fewer people felt they could afford to replace their vacuum cleaners. Having a new product helped them to maintain sales revenue.

Market change

What makes markets change, sometimes fast? Incomes may rise in a boom or fall in a recession. But many other things can happen in the marketplace, as businesses look to obtain a competitive advantage. They may:

● Come up with their own new products or variants.

● Cut prices and maybe costs as well.

● Start advertising campaigns with attention-grabbing features that excite customers' interest.

● Offer incentives to customers and distributors.

Every time something changes, all competitors in the market will have to review their marketing objectives and adapt the marketing mix to avoid losing market share and sales revenue. The component parts of the marketing mix have to be carefully co-ordinated so that they focus on the needs of the specific situation. One or two elements of the 4 Ps may become particularly important – for example, if someone comes up with a new and more versatile mobile phone, the competing business which thought it was doing nicely with its own version will have to redesign its own product if it is to stay in the market.

Special tip
You will have to do the same if you are asked about the marketing mix. Look carefully at the context and suggest a marketing mix which meets the requirements for the particular market or business you are asked about.

The product life cycle

Sugar refiners might think that demand for their product will go on for ever, even though health warnings may be a threat and require them to monitor the situation. But the need to figure out likely product life is probably much more serious in the fashion market, or in the market for consumer electronics such as iPods, iPhones and computer tablets.

The product life cycle (plc) tries to gauge the progress of a particular product in terms of its sales in its anticipated life time. Most products pass through six stages – development, introduction, growth, maturity, saturation and decline. Some products, for example the technologically advanced ones from Dyson, will have huge development costs and many prototypes may not make the introduction stage.

Product life cycle

When introducing novelty products to meet the demands of a particular craze, a life span of months may be regarded as a success, so long as the promotion of such a product can be geared to achieving quick sales. For other products a period of up to ten years might be seen as a required life cycle. Whatever the product, it is important to map its actual progress against its anticipated progress in order to respond with marketing strategies such as promotions or product enhancements to boost sales: these are known as **extension strategies**.

Figure 2: Basic product life cycle

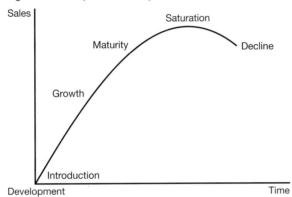

Figure 2 represents a basic product life cycle. Development costs, which may be significant, are incurred before the product is introduced to the market. These costs may have arisen over a number of years. As the product is introduced money will be earned from sales. During the growth period sales will rise and a profit will hopefully be made. There is no exact point at which this will occur. A number of factors will influence this, such as the profit on each item; the amount spent on research and the extent and cost of the marketing campaign.

Extension strategies

The **product life cycle** refers to the phases that most products go through between their first introduction to the market and their eventual decline in sales, which may lead to production ceasing.

An **extension strategy** is a way of increasing sales by relaunching the product with a new image, or aiming at a different market segment and promoted in fresh ways.

Figure 3: Short product life cycle

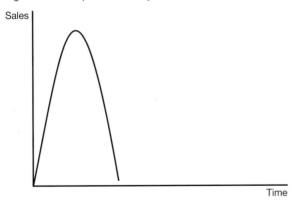

Figure 3 illustrates the life cycle of a product that is regarded as a fad, a product with a very short life. Toys associated with a television character may fall into this category, as will a technology product that is quickly superseded by a more advanced product. Platform trainers might be a good example.

When sales reach maturity level, an extension strategy may be used in a number of different ways:

- finding new markets for the product
- finding new uses for the product
- bringing out associated products to boost the original market
- changing the shape or packaging of a product
- changing the specification or components of the product to suit specific markets
- persuading customers to use the product more frequently.

Figure 4: Extended product life cycle

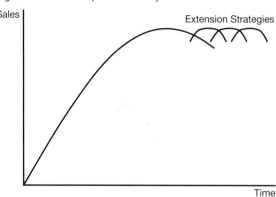

This could be as simple as changing the packaging or as complex as redesigning the product. In the case of the Harry Potter stories, a number of books were written; these can be viewed as the original product. The films could be viewed as an extension strategy, a huge one in this case. When toys, games and clothing are introduced you have an extension strategy which will keep product sales growing for a number of years. Figure 4 shows how the product life cycle may be extended.

Even extremely large firms will not always risk introducing a product across a large market at one time. Cadbury (now part of Kraft) have often trialled new products in one part of the country, to gauge demand before releasing them onto the whole market. Some products take a while to take hold in the market, some never do and some appear to be an instant success.

The market for mobile phones is one of the fastest moving of all consumer technology products. With sales in the millions of units each year and with new applications being added frequently, each item in the product range must be carefully monitored. Using the plc is one way of doing this. Firms may target a particular anticipated life cycle for their product, aiming to achieve a short term goal or a longer life. The marketing mix is a key element in any launch process – as in the case of Lucozade.

Lucozade

The firm Lucozade was originally established in 1927 and created the drink as a pick-me-up for those suffering from illnesses such as flu. The most common place to buy it was the chemist. Now it is a classic example of a product that redefined itself – as a sports drink. By the 1980s, Lucozade was part of Glaxo Smith Kline's range and they wanted to re-think its marketing mix. A concerted campaign was launched to re-brand the drink as one for healthy people; indeed the promotion was centred on the healthiest of people such as sportsmen and women and those who had just completed strenuous physical workouts. The logo was modernised, the packaging changed dramatically and Lucozade was sold through supermarkets and convenience stores. There are few companies that can boast such an amazing and successful turnaround.

Place the products in the left column in one (or more) of the marketing mix categories listed on the right. You may think that some products fall into more than one category, so there are no right and wrong answers but plenty of scope for discussion.

Lucozade	New product use
The Mini (car)	Associated product
Breakfast cereals	Changed packaging
Sportswear clothing	Changed specification/components
Books	More frequent product use
Lego	New market for existing product
Mobile phones	Different distribution strategies
Coca-Cola	
Trainers	
Harry Potter toys	

When growth starts to flatten out firms must be prepared to make key decisions on their product's longevity. By the time a product has reached the maturity stage it may be too late to breathe life back into it, especially if the specification needs changing. A judgement must be made as to when to re-invent a product or service, whether to market it more extensively or whether to stop promoting it and discontinue production.

Before adopting an extension strategy or seeking to bring out associated products, businesses need to assess their production capabilities, considering whether they can actually expand production successfully. Established firms are better able to decide this than young businesses, but even they can get caught out by unexpected levels of demand. One of the reasons why seemingly strong firms go bust is their inability to gauge the level of demand correctly, sometimes accepting orders that they can't fulfil and sometimes overtrading, i.e. expanding without having sufficient working capital. They may face cash flow problems if sales revenues are delayed.

The product portfolio

Product portfolio

Chocolate

Cadbury's has hundreds of brands. Now and then one will be discontinued, but there are not so many of these. Here are just a few, with their launch dates:

Dairy Milk   1905, their best selling product by 1913

Creme egg   1923

Fruit and Nut 1928

Whole Nut   1933

Wispa   1983.

Cadbury doesn't rely entirely on its old favourites. The launch adverts for the Wispa bar said 'Have you heard the Wispa?'. Comedy stars from Dad's Army and the like appeared in the TV ads. For some time the Wispa sold well. But when it appeared to be moving out of saturation and into decline, in 2003, it was discontinued.

By that time, on-line communications were developing well and what followed was a massive resurrection campaign by disappointed customers. At first Cadbury ignored it as being too much of a niche protest. But it went on – and on, soon moving to Facebook. Wispa fans stormed the stage at Glastonbury, trying to get the bar back. In 2007 Cadbury tried a limited run of 20 million; it had sold out within a few weeks. In 2008 they brought it back – for good, they said. They call it 'the people's chocolate bar'.

In 2010, Cadbury launched the Wispa Duo and asked customers "which side do you prefer. Is it the left bar because it tastes so leftie, or the right bar because it's so, well…right?"

Questions

1. Why do you think Cadbury launched the Wispa Duo?
2. How likely do you think it is that the Wispa will last as long as Dairy Milk has?
3. Would you expect the marketing mix for the Duo to change over time? Explain why, and give examples of how it might change.

Businesses that have had time to develop usually have a range of products, sometimes all of a similar nature but quite often, very varied in nature. Together, these products are known as the **product portfolio**. Businesses like to balance their portfolios so that they can attract as big a market as possible. Obviously some will be mass marketing but many of these also produce for certain niche markets, where they can find profitable opportunities.

> The **product portfolio** is the full range of products sold by the business. It will usually be carefully designed to reach as many market segments as possible. Portfolio analysis is used to position products so that together, they attract as much of the potential market as possible.

Cadbury has a huge range of chocolate products but is also big in ice cream, cakes, biscuits and drinks. It keeps up its old favourites but it also discontinues products that are not selling well enough to make a good profit. Keeping its product portfolio under continuous review is an important task for the management. Like most companies it tries to balance its portfolio so that it always has products in every stage of the product life cycle.

The Boston Matrix

Developed by the Boston Consulting Group, the Boston Matrix is an attempt to analyse the product portfolio of a firm. It defines the stage in its life that a product is in. Products are placed in four categories according to market share and market growth. The categories of Star, Cash Cow, Problem Child (or Question Mark) and Dog are set out in Figure 5.

Cash cows

- Star products have a high market share of a high growth market, for example the Kindle.

- Cash Cows are those products which have a good stable market share and generate funds on a regular basis. Cadbury's Dairy Milk chocolate is a good example.

- Problem children are products that have not sold well so far but have potential for growth, e.g. the electric car.

- Dogs are products that are in decline. They may have had a good market share in the past but another product has superseded them, for example the Sony Walkman.

Figure 5: The Boston Matrix

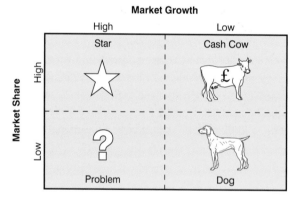

Cash flow and marketing

Cash flow

Cash cows are highly profitable. Stars may be profitable too but they have to cover the development costs. These may be very high, and if they are it will be some time before a star becomes truly worthwhile. Of course there is no question about the Kindle, but other slightly less successful products may take longer to cover all their costs.

Problem children usually need more money spent on them to make them profitable. Dogs, by their nature, will be losing money. When businesses use the Boston Matrix to analyse their portfolios, they will conclude that dogs must be discontinued as soon as sales revenue is below the break-even level.

Cash cows and stars will produce a positive cash flow. This can be used to invest in the problem children. A relaunch or an extension strategy may be appropriate but this can be costly and involve all aspects of the marketing mix.

Boston matrix

Show what you know

This exercise can be carried out individually, in pairs or in small groups, depending on the amount of research to be carried out. Listed below is a range of cars available from Toyota. (Some Toyotas have had technical problems leading to product recall but that is not the purpose of this exercise and should be ignored.) First, place each of the brands in one of the four boxes of the Boston Matrix. Then carry out your research and draw up a second Boston Matrix and place the cars in the boxes you now think they should be in. Are there many differences? Was your initial perception correct? Are there cars in each of the four categories?

Toyota car models:

Avensis	Prius
Yaris	AYGO
Auris	Verso
Rav 4	Urban Cruiser
Land Cruiser	iQ

Question

Based on your findings what advice would you give Toyota on how to manage their product mix?

When answering the above question, consider this: will Toyota have enough production capacity to carry out your recommendations? What will be the financial implications of your recommendations? Are there any weaknesses in the Boston model?

Is an increase in market share the 'be all and end all' for firms aiming to be successful? Critics of the Boston Matrix believe that it focuses too much on market growth, to the detriment of consolidation. Other strategies should perhaps be pursued. The criticism is valid if a business chooses to examine their product mix with just the one technique. However, combined with other approaches, e.g. the product life cycle, it can be a useful way to devise marketing objectives and strategies.

Special tip

When answering questions, be careful to analyse the merits of the product life cycle in some detail. As well as being a predictor of the broad pattern of sales, both in units and value, the plc can be used to pinpoint when new products may need launching. Along with the Boston Matrix it can be used by some firms to manage the product portfolio. It can help to pinpoint the level of sales at which a product will come into profit and it can be used to help a business make the decision to discontinue the product.

Chapter 3 **Branding and patents**

Brands

Frank C. Mars started making confectionery products in 1911 in the US. His son Forrest came to the UK, rented a factory in Slough in 1932 and invented the Mars Bar. In 1959 advertisers came up with the slogan, 'A Mars a day helps you work, rest and play'. Later it was rebranded with the slogan 'Pleasure you can't measure', designed to attract younger, feminine customers. The company is still family owned.

Extension strategies included smaller 'Fun time' and 'Snack time' bars, sold in multiple packs. Then came the highly successful ice cream bar. The basic recipe is the same today, although the arrangement of the component ingredients was changed in 2002. Purist enthusiasts protested vigorously.

Questions

1. Why do so many businesses strive to create a recognisable brand? You should be able to state and explain at least three good reasons.

2. Why do people stay loyal to many of the brands they buy? Explain giving at least three examples of your own.

Brand loyalty

Branding distinguishes a product from its competitors. A **brand name** makes it recognisable. Once customers have identified the desirable features of the product, a reputation will build up; customers will get a sense of the reliability of the product in terms of quality. In time, branding adds to the status of the product, giving it added value. **Brand loyalty** – the tendency of customers to make repeat purchases of their favourite brands – can make successful brands very valuable indeed. Often, the brands a business has developed are the key attraction in a takeover bid. (This was a major factor in the Kraft takeover of Cadbury in 2010.) A brand leader (the brand with the largest market share) will become extremely valuable.

Brands enhance competitive advantage. They may do this by having product refinements that are very attractive. But they may also differentiate themselves by involving a level of personal service that customers appreciate. This might come from after-sales service for manufactured goods or it might be an important element in a service product. But of course whatever the tangible benefits of the product might be, branding is designed to create an image too, one that suits the buyers in the market segment for which the product is designed. What, would you say, defines the Mars brand?

Brand recognition is usually vastly enhanced by advertising. Product differentiation is important too – brands depend on being recognisably different but branding itself helps to make them so. So it is not surprising that branding is a key element in the marketing mix. Firms spend an extraordinary amount of money on getting their brand right. They target certain markets and sub-sets of markets and devise brands that will be especially likely to appeal within those markets. In fact branding is integral to the marketing effort.

Product placement, sometimes called embedded marketing, means displaying the product in a non-advertising context, e.g. a film or a TV programme or possibly mentioning it in a book. This used to be illegal in the UK but the ban was lifted early in 2011. So now, if you see someone on TV holding a branded product, it may be that the business that owns the brand has paid for that product to be there.

Brand names create an identity for the product and highlight the ways in which it is different from competing products.

Brand loyalty refers to the way in which customers will make repeat purchases when they have decided that they prefer the product to others. Some brand loyalty reflects customers' clear preferences, but it can also be a result of inertia. When this happens, the brand's position may be threatened by lively advertising of other products.

Branding

A brand might be one product, a range of products or the actual business itself (think of Nike or Adidas). Branding often allows businesses to charge a higher price than those of competing products. Of course, they will have to work at maintaining the relative desirability of the product; usually this means that they will need to continue advertising throughout the life of the product and they may need to look at 'place' aspects of the marketing mix, to ensure that their product is very visible. Brands can get involved in aggressive price cutting but this does not often happen.

Brands and sponsorship

In a world where celebrity culture is 'king', businesses pay huge sums of money to celebrities to endorse their brand. But firms have to be wary about what they do with their brand and with whom they wish to be associated. Given the importance of reputation in preserving brand loyalty, mistakes can be costly.

Consider the following three examples:

- **Manchester United** has signed a deal worth £40m over 4 years with DHL, the logistics company, for sponsorship of their training kit – not match day kit. Match day kit is sponsored to the tune of £20m a year by Aon, the US financial giant.

- **Tiger Woods**, the golfer, lost lucrative sponsorship deals with Tag Heuer, the luxury watch brand, and Gillette, among others, as details of his private life hit the headlines. It has been estimated that his sponsors lost revenue of over £2bn as a result of Woods' association with their products.

- **Abercrombie & Fitch**, an up-market clothing firm are reported to have offered a considerable sum of money to Mike Sorrentino, one of the stars of the MTV reality show Jersey Shore, not to wear its clothes. The show, now in its fourth season, is wildly popular with the young demographic that buy Abercrombie & Fitch clothes. The company issued a statement saying "We understand that the show is for entertainment purposes, but believe this association is contrary to the aspirational nature of our brand, and may be distressing to many of our fans."

A helping hand – patents and trademarks

Many people come into business having previously been employed by someone else in the same line of work. They may feel they have the expertise to do a better job or they may decide to branch out on their own as they have spotted a gap in the market. However, their ability to research the market may be limited; their ability to carry out research and development (R&D) prior to entering a market may be still more so. The time and finance needed would be very hard to obtain. Many first time entrepreneurs have to develop their ideas in their own time, using their own savings.

In these circumstances it is desperately important for the innovative entrepreneur to be able to protect his or her idea. That 'give and take' may be achieved if the law on preserving the benefits of an invention is firmly in place to reward the inventor and to prevent copying. In the UK the laws on patents and copyright, plus those on trademarks, attempt to do this.

Established companies often have R&D departments and are continuously improving

Copyright and patents allow innovative entrepreneurs to protect their ideas.

their products and processes, as well as inventing completely new products. They too need an incentive to invest in this way. Their research will give them a competitive advantage but this would not last long if anyone could copy their ideas. It would not be long enough for them to recoup their development costs.

Intellectual property rights

Where a new invention is involved, individuals and businesses can apply to the Intellectual Property Office (IPO) for a patent. (This used to be called the Patent Office.) This will give them twenty years during which no one will be allowed to copy their invention. The IPO often takes two or more years to process the application, but nevertheless, patents do give a considerable degree of protection. For the duration of the patent, its owner will be able to make money from using it in its products or production processes.

A **patent** protects the functionality of a product in terms of how it works and its application. Once granted, the patent gives the owner the right to prevent others from producing, importing or selling their invention, without prior permission. The owner of the patent will be able to sue anyone who infringes it in the courts.

In the UK there is a fee of between £230 – £280 for a patent, and after 4 years an annual renewal fee. Notice that patents are granted for new ways of producing, as well as for new products or components. We can distinguish two types of innovation – **product innovation** where new products are involved, and **process innovation** where there are new machines or procedures have been developed in order to cut production costs. L'Oréal, below, is all about product innovation.

Product innovation involves inventing or designing new or improved products, such as Dyson's bladeless fan.

Process innovation involves the use of new technologies in the production process and may play a big part in cutting costs. Robots are just one example.

L'Oréal

The cosmetics giant is famous for holding a massive collection of patents. In 2009, it had nearly 2000 in the US alone. (Although Gillette has even more for its shaving products.) Its brand image is partly based on innovative enhancements of its products so their actual composition is an important aspect of the L'Oréal marketing effort. The product range is huge because L'Oréal owns Lancôme, Armani, Ralph Lauren, Yves Saint Laurent, Diesel, Redken, Helena Rubinstein and Kerastase, amongst many other brands.

Each brand is aimed at a different market segment. Every time the company finds a formulation that works, it patents it. The company believes that research and development are critical to its success.

Questions

1. Why would R&D be important for a company producing hair-care and cosmetic products?

2. Why is patent protection important to L'Oréal?

3. Why are brand names widely used for these products? Why does L'Oréal have separate names for its different brand ranges?

Patents can be registered internationally. Venture capital funds that support small businesses that have come up with an exciting invention expect international patents to be in place before they provide finance. Businesses that want to copy an invention during the life of the patent will have to find a new and different way of designing and making it.

Microsoft goes to considerable lengths to ensure no-one copies their products.

Copyright

Patents are part of **intellectual property rights** (IPRs). These include copyright, which gives legal protection to authors, composers and artists. These people do not have to register because their work is protected from copying by law and infringements can be prosecuted in the courts. Their protection lasts for the lifetime of the author plus 70 years. It is not clear whether copyright protection will be so helpful to authors in the future if many more books become available from cheap or free digital sources.

Copyright applies to many kinds of written word, including Microsoft products! One reason why these are expensive is that Microsoft goes to considerable lengths to ensure that no one copies them, and then sells them at a high price. This is a kind of monopoly. But you can see that the complex programming of an up to date gaming programme would be very costly and if it were not protected, it might be that no one would have an incentive to make it available.

In the music business something different has happened. Illegal downloading has eaten into CD sales to a dramatic extent and many bands are having to go on tour in order to make any money at all. It would be very difficult to pursue all illegal downloaders through the courts, although it is often pointed out that they are actually stealing the music. It is not clear how this situation will develop in the future so watch out for news about the music industry. It would be a pity if the end result were to involve much less choice of recorded music, which would be against the interests of consumers.

Show what you know

1. Think carefully about what your view of intellectual property rights would be if you were:
   (a) part of a new band that is just becoming popular
   (b) an author whose first book is about to be published
   (c) an engineering design student with a brilliant idea
   (d) a consumer who likes to listen to music and read books and buy cheap cosmetics.

2. For many years Glaxo Smith Kline made enormous profits from sales of Zantac, a drug that controlled stomach ulcers. Then the patent lapsed.
   (a) What do you think happened next?
   (b) Eventually, Zantac was relicensed as an over-the-counter product, for sale without prescription. GSK repositioned it as an indigestion remedy. Why would this make sense for GSK?

Patents and copyrights give people and businesses with original ideas a monopoly – only they can sell the product they have devised. The protection this gives creates the incentive needed to innovate and produce original work.

> **Intellectual property rights** are acquired by people and businesses when they hold patents or copyright. They protect them from competition so that they can recoup the cost of creating their products.
>
> **Copyright** gives legal protection against copying to authors, composers and artists. Infringements can be pursued through legal action.

Trademarks

The UK Intellectual Property Office defines a trademark as 'a sign which can distinguish your goods or services from those of your competitors'. It can be for example words, logos or a combination of both. It must be registered with the IPO; for this it must be unique in terms of its design. This gives it a life span of 10 years. The cost for a single trademark in the UK is at present £60. Trademarks and logos are very much a part of branding and always have been, because they make the brand easy to recognise.

Trademarks

The Beatles

In 1968 Apple Corps was set up by the Beatles to release their songs and manage their creative affairs. In 1976 the American technology firm Apple Inc was formed. A dispute between the two firms developed in 1980, when the late George Harrison noticed an advert for Apple computers in a magazine. He felt there was potential for trademark conflict between the two firms. The sides reached a deal in 1981 allowing Apple Computers to use the name as long as it stuck to computers, while the Beatles' company would continue in the entertainment field.

Apple Corps

But as computers developed and their musical capabilities grew, the sides ended up in court again in 1989, resulting in a new deal. They clashed again when Apple Inc launched the iTunes download store in 2003, with the record label claiming the computer firm had encroached on its territory again. The case ended up in court in 2006.

The final deal agreed on was that Apple Inc would take full control of the Apple brand and license certain trademarks back to the Beatles' record company, Apple Corps, for continued use.

Source: Adapted from a BBC News Channel item 5 February 2007

Questions

1. Could the Beatles have lost money in the period 1976-80, as a result of Apple Inc's activities? Explain your thinking on this.

2. In your opinion, had the situation changed by 2006? In what ways?

It is likely that the most satisfied people at the end of the process would have been the lawyers. While the dispute was running the Beatles' songs were not available on any legal download service, but the truce has paved the way for the songs to appear on the iTunes download store. Similar disputes are commonplace but few, if any, will have such high profile players.

Chapter 4

Choosing a price

The café

Kaye Walker owned two cafés in the market town of Beverley in East Yorkshire. There were a number of competing businesses nearby and any changes in price would need to take this into account. But food prices were rising so even though she was buying at wholesale prices, her costs were rising. She decided to increase her prices, by an average of 5 per cent. There was a slight reduction in trade at one of the cafés but no discernible reduction in trade at the other.

In general, having competitors close by, who did not increase their prices, should have led to a transfer of trade to Kaye's rivals. After all, substitute products were available and they were convenient.

Questions

1. Explain reasons why, after price rises at her cafés, Kaye Walker did not see a significant change in demand for her products.

2. Discuss, given the effect on demand after a price increase, whether Kaye should increase prices again.

Price and value

Price is a very important element in the marketing mix and may have a critical effect on sales revenue. Small businesses like Kaye's may just think of it in terms of finding the price that customers will actually be willing to pay, sometimes described as 'what the market will bear'. This in turn has a lot to do with how much competition there is. But then if costs rise, the small business will want to pass this increase on to the customer if they can. This will depend in turn on whether the customer feels that in spite of the price increase, the product is still good value for money.

Bigger businesses are likely to have differentiated products that command a degree of customer loyalty. If customers have decided that a particular product offers the best value for money because it meets their needs precisely, they are likely to be less sensitive to price increases. Businesses with famous brands will be in an even better position: the more highly esteemed the brand is, the more loyalty it will have.

The need to preserve customer loyalty by offering value for money should be kept in mind by everyone, no matter what the size of the business. And this will mean that a price change will usually entail an all round review of the marketing mix. Businesses that are selling products with no distinctive features (sometimes called commodity products) compete entirely on price; this would apply to porridge oats and iron ore. But for most products there is an element of **non-price competition** – involving product design, promotion and place.

Non-price competition involves adding value to the product by finding ways to make it different from competing products. Design, quality, unique features, advertising, packaging and other forms of promotion may all be possible.

Businesses can benefit from careful market positioning. (Go back to Unit 1 if you need to revise this.) For example, Kaye might have been able to differentiate the products on her menu. Then people who were most likely to be put off by increased prices would still be able to find something basic but reasonably priced, while others might choose a meal at a higher price.

Every business has its own story to tell on pricing. Only a few can decide on prices in the way Arsenal does (overleaf).

Price sensitivity

Arsenal

When Arsenal football club used to play at Highbury in North London they would fill their ground every game. In fact over the last 5 years or so at that venue (before they moved to the Emirates stadium in 2006) they could have filled their ground with season ticket holders, but they didn't. They limited the number of season ticket holders to between 22,000 and 23,000. They did this because they knew that they could easily sell the remaining tickets at higher prices closer to the match date. Season ticket holders get their passes at a discounted rate.

The value of this to the club is that the revenue from season passes is received prior to the start of the season and can be spent on player acquisition. Arsenal, under Arsène Wenger, became so successful that they needed more seats and they eventually moved to a 60,000 seat stadium which is sold out for most games. At the old ground they could have put the price of their tickets up by 5, 10 or even 15 percent and demand would have remained the same.

Questions

1. Why were fans so unconcerned about ticket prices that they were willing to pay more without reducing the number of tickets they bought?

2. What might happen that would change this situation?

Price elasticity

When it is possible for businesses to raise prices without losing many of their customers, demand for the product is said to be price inelastic. For a business, knowing how customers will respond to price changes is very important. There is a way of measuring the impact of a change in prices – using the idea of **price elasticity of demand**. It has a formula:

$$\text{Price elasticity of demand (PED)} = \frac{\% \text{ change in quantity demanded}}{\% \text{ change in price}}$$

If prices are raised by 10%, and quantity sold falls only by 5%, the PED will be -0.5. Demand is inelastic. If on the other hand a price cut of 5% leads to sales increasing by 10%, then it is -2 and demand is elastic. Basic foods like bread typically have price inelastic demand. Exotic foods e.g. mangoes will have price elastic demand.

> **Price elasticity of demand** measures the change in quantity sold that results from a change in price. If it is zero, the price change has no effect. Between zero and -1, demand is inelastic. If it goes beyond -1, say to -2, demand is elastic, i.e. very sensitive to changes in price.

In fact football clubs in the English Premier League have become (in the main) quite sophisticated operators. A number of clubs price tickets differently depending on the opposition. It is not uncommon for clubs to have three bands of prices; a high price to reflect the reputation and aura of clubs such as Manchester United and Liverpool; a middle band for clubs such as Aston Villa and Everton, and a third band for clubs

Milk

Summer Holidays

Cigarettes

Is demand price elastic or inelastic for each of these?

who are new to the league or have a lower support base such as Blackburn Rovers and Wigan Athletic. Clubs know the likely demand for tickets at certain prices for certain games and price accordingly, yet it is unlikely you will hear them talk about the price elasticity of demand for their product.

Small businesses can set prices appropriately just by keeping in close touch with their markets. Most will never have heard of PED. Larger businesses are likely to have people working full time on market research. They can collect data that will allow them to estimate the PED for each of their products. This will give them a good understanding on which to base their pricing strategy.

Choosing a price

Pricing strategies

All businesses should have a marketing plan and part of that plan should consider the pricing strategies open to them. In general, businesses with few competitors and therefore a large share of the market will face inelastic demand for their product; an increase in price will not lead to a proportionate fall in demand. Revenue will increase when price increases.

Businesses that have only a small share of the market face many competitors, each with a similar product. The demand for their product is usually highly elastic. In these circumstances, raising prices, say by 5 per cent, will lead to a more than proportionate fall in demand for its products because buyers will turn to substitute products. Total revenue will fall as price rises. Conversely if price is cut by 5 per cent then demand should rise by more than 5 per cent as long as competitors don't respond in a similar fashion. But this may well happen and if it does, there could be a price war.

To understand the impact of price changes on sales revenue you need a simple example.

Business A is selling its computers at £400 each and selling 200 per week. Demand is elastic at -2, because there are several other computer suppliers in the area. They increase their price to £440, a 10% rise. So sales go down by 20%, to 160.

Before the price increase, sales revenue is 200 x £400 = £80,000.

After the price increase, sales revenue is 160 x £440 = £70,400.

Business A will not have solved its problems. If it had known its elasticity of demand beforehand it might have avoided the mistaken decision. In general, any pricing decision requires a full, up-to-date understanding of the market and usually, some extra market research. Figure 6 shows how a business might think through the possibilities.

Price sensitivity

Figure 6: What about a price increase?

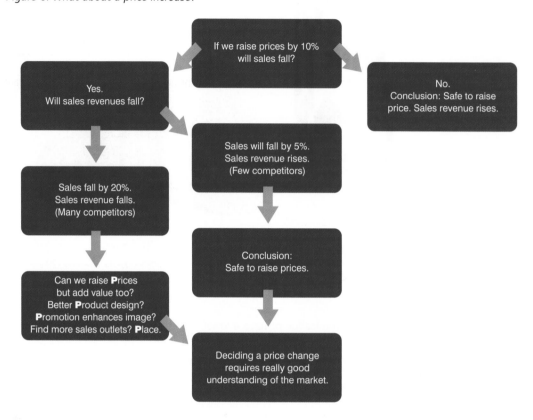

Show what you know

1. Business B is in the same market as business A, selling the same quantity at the same price, with PED equal to -2. But it tries a different strategy. It cuts prices by 10% in an attempt to sell more. Work out what will happen to its sales revenue.

2. Now look at Business C which sells Louis Vuitton bags for £150 each. Sales are normally 100 per week. There are no other sellers in that city and PED is -0.5. It raises prices by 10%. What will happen to sales revenue?

3. Fulham FC increased the price of their cheapest season ticket for 2011-12 from £285 to £379. If as a result of this demand fell by 15 per cent, what is the price elasticity of demand of this product? Show your calculations.

4. Should Fulham have raised their prices? Discuss.

5. How does branding affect a product's price elasticity?

Chapter 5

Social trends and the marketing mix

Ethical business

"The business of business should not just be about money, it should be about responsibility. It should be about the public good, not private greed."

Dame Anita Roddick, Human Rights activist, Founder of the Body Shop

Anita Roddick was not the only successful entrepreneur to bring some social awareness to the private sector. After all such a philanthropist and social reformer as Robert Owen, was renowned for his excellent treatment of his workers in Scotland's New Lanark Mills as far back as the 18th century. Owen was a socialist whose greatest work was in the protection of children. In the 19th century Joseph Rowntree was another pioneering philanthropist in the UK and the Cadbury family went as far as setting up a village for the company's employees at Bourneville in the Midlands. Many other notable business people have given huge amounts of their time and money more recently to good causes (e.g. Bill Gates), but none are more closely associated with social awareness within business than Anita Roddick.

Some say that Roddick's links to Greenpeace, to the Big Issue, the campaign 'Against Animal Testing', to Fair Trade, were all just a cunning ploy to entice shoppers to the firms' products. (The same has been said about Body Shop's campaigning since Roddick's death, in 2007, on the issues of HIV and Aids.) But of course she had no need to go to the great lengths she did in order to be successful in business.

Questions

1. To what extent do you think that greater public awareness of social trends has encouraged businesses to adopt ethical trading practices?

2. Why do many businesses include ethical trading as one of their objectives?

Stakeholders

A **stakeholder** can be any person or group of people who have an interest in a particular business. Owners and shareholders are stakeholders along with employees; so also are the local community, suppliers, customers and the government. This might not be so obvious when a firm starts up but is perhaps more apparent when a firm shuts down.

> **Stakeholders** are all those individuals and groups that may be affected by the actions of the business concerned.
>
> **Business responsibility**, or **ethical business**, or **corporate social responsibility**, involves taking decisions in a way that respects all stakeholders' interests. Ethical business practices include sustainable sourcing of inputs, avoiding environmental degradation (e.g. by polluting), prioritising employee welfare and offering customers and suppliers a fair deal.

Many businesses recognise that stakeholders' views should be taken into account. But not all do! Some say that the primary objective for any business is to make a profit for the owners or shareholders. Of course, they will say, the business must act within the law of the country where it is doing business. Many would claim that making a profit ultimately benefits all stakeholders.

In the past, many businesses created a great deal of pollution which they did not attempt to clean up. Mining companies particularly had a very destructive effect on their local environments. Many people lived and worked in unhealthy conditions for very low pay. Stricter laws and regulations have now improved the situation greatly in developed countries but low income countries lag far behind.

Ethical trading

Some people have always been disturbed by this but nowadays most people expect higher standards. Many businesses have responded by trying to establish a reputation for ethical trading. Some businesses do actually make changes to the way they produce, market and distribute their products. McDonald's say that since 2007, 80% of all packaging used by them in the UK was made from renewable resources. But do they mean recycled paper or wood from sustainable forests? And did this actually reduce the environmental impact of the packaging?

When reputations are at stake, all businesses look again at their marketing mix. Some have found that using sustainably produced inputs is cheaper in the long run. Many have found that they can reduce their energy costs by looking for ways to use less. Publicising these changes can be used to help promote the company's products as environmentally friendly. Nike tried this, with only partial success.

Nike

Nike, one of the world's leading sportswear sellers, with a famous global brand, contracts out most of its production to independent local suppliers in a number of East Asian countries. The primary objective is to keep down production costs. Over the last 20 years there has been a concerted campaign to expose the maltreatment of employees and the sweatshop conditions in these factories. According to Vietnam Labour Watch, "Nike did not pay minimum wages, did not provide proper working conditions and did not take adequate health and safety measure." It was also accused of turning a blind eye to the use of child labour and sexual harassment in its factories. In addition, according to the report, Nike's own code of conduct was being violated consistently by its contractors.

Nike has consistently denied that it used unfair labour practices. The company sent representatives to colleges in the US in an attempt to convince students that Nike's treatment of foreign workers was fair. In addition they targeted journalists in countries in which they had factories to report their side of the story. Vada Manager, Nike's senior spokesperson, explained the rationale for this move. "Unlike US based reporters, who are writing about factories they have never visited, journalists working in those countries understand the local conditions." Nike offered a 12 minute online video tour of its contracted shoe facilities in Vietnam.

In May 2001, a report prepared by a labour rights group claimed that even after three years, Nike had not delivered on its promises. There is still concern, some years on, that Nike was not doing enough to protect its employees, with reports that its own factory managers were being warned about internal company inspections in advance, so as to minimise problems.

Source: Adapted from Business Ethics Case Studies IBS Center for Management Research

Questions

1. How could Nike use its marketing mix to explain more about its treatment of workers in Asia?
2. What is ethical trading?
3. How might a firm such as Primark use the marketing mix to counteract allegations of unethical trading?
4. Why would firms spend a great deal of time and money explaining how they obtained raw materials from sustainable sources?
5. Why have some British supermarkets promoted a reduction in the use of plastic carrier bags on their web sites and in other publicity materials?

Business and the local community

A family-owned bakery in the small town where I live shut down recently. It had been trading for over 100 years. Probably the main reason for closure was competition from supermarkets, with their bulk purchasing power and their ability to keep overheads relatively low. They are able to sell at much lower prices than the smaller bakery. But customers of the bakery lose out, particularly the elderly and those who can't drive.

Supporting the local community

Of course the supermarket now offers a delivery service. But the local community loses out as choice is reduced; a reason for going to the town square is removed and probably custom for other nearby shops is lost. Suppliers lose a client and the government loses revenue from taxation of profits. Even the local authority will lose out as revenue from business rates falls. Employees lose their jobs, putting extra strain on public finances as job seekers' allowance payments increase. The unemployed cut back on their purchases of luxuries and other businesses suffer loss of trade. There is a vicious circle. This bakery supported local fairs and events and those activities therefore lost revenue.

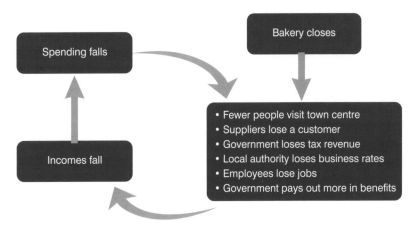

There are counter arguments to this. Large businesses would say that:

● they often contribute to the local economy through sponsorships and training and charitable donations.

● their size and market power allows them to dictate low prices to their suppliers (many of which will be comparatively small businesses that depend on them as customers). This helps them to keep their costs down and charge low prices to customers.

BAe Systems has a factory employing over 2,000 workers in Brough, East Yorkshire. It provides an additional fire station to help out locally. BAe argue that their free parking for employees saves them money, and of course they pump money into the local economy, either directly by purchasing supplies, or indirectly when their employees spend money locally. They also claim to have green credentials.

It may be difficult for a manufacturer of aircraft to convince communities that they are ethical traders but they will argue that they source sustainable materials and that the trees they plant around the factory to reduce noise lead to reduced carbon emissions. Many businesses are required by local authorities to provide facilities for the community as a condition of receiving planning permission to expand.

Show what you know

Identify a local business that has taken an ethical stance on a particular issue. Say why you think it did this, in as much detail as you can.

Food miles

Worries about food miles

Some foods travel a long way to get to their customers. Their transport requires fossil fuels and will create greenhouse gases.

● Is it ethical to eat food that was produced thousands of miles away? How badly do we need fruit from the southern hemisphere, or tuna from the Indian Ocean?

This is a controversial question. Of course it is true that if all food was produced close to its market, there would be lower greenhouse gas emissions. But in order to produce some foodstuffs efficiently, you need the right climate. Kenya has a good climate for growing green beans. Many jobs have been created there and as a result, many people have had better incomes. This matters because in Kenya, many people live on very little.

● So ought we to avoid eating Kenyan green beans? This is a tough one. What would then happen to the jobs created in Kenya and the incomes of the people who are contributing to production?

Do you feel you could actually buy much more of the food you eat from UK producers? Do you look to see where your favourite foods come from? They might cost more if produced in the UK.

● Could you pay a bit more? Could you grow food in your own garden, perhaps?

As you can see, worries about food miles raise many questions. Finding a good marketing mix for imported foods is not difficult. But would it be ethical?

Internet
sales

Online retailing

Table 1: Internet sales as a percentage of total retail sales

	%
January 2007	3.0
January 2008	4.8
January 2009	6.6
January 2010	7.6
January 2011	8.9
July 2011	9.1

Source: The Office for National Statistics

These figures are extraordinary and pose many questions for traditional retail outlets. Many businesses with traditional stores have embraced changing technology and changing social habits and have become part of the shop-at-home culture, whilst many new businesses use only online selling to sell their products and services. Among the traditionalists who have embraced this most recent of trends are the leading supermarket groups and clothes retailers. Banks and financial service providers are keen for their customers to open online accounts as this move will reduce their costs for those organisations. This leaves them with the opportunity to make increased profits for their shareholders or to pass on savings as price reductions to their customers.

Among the winners in this revolution in shopping are the logistics firms who deliver the goods. Among the losers will be those who are affected by increasing traffic loads and increasing congestion.

The Oldest Sweet Shop in England has embraced online retailing.

Online selling and the marketing mix

Businesses that have decided to retail online are faced with the challenge of how to adapt their marketing mix to achieve best results. The product itself may or may not change. For example cafés and restaurants that will cater for outside functions, delivering to the door, are unlikely to change what they have on offer – only the setting is changed. But firms that want to cater for the world market may have to make significant changes, perhaps to their product but also in relation to promotion and getting their product to its destination. Web-site design may be critical in attracting customers, but there must also be a strategy for making sure potential customers can find it. This may require conventional advertising.

An online business

The oldest sweet shop in England is The Oldest Sweet Shop in England! Established in 1827 in the picturesque Yorkshire Dales, you can buy sherberts and liquorice, toffee and chocolate, all produced by small independent suppliers. But in 2005 The Oldest Sweet Shop in England Online was founded. You can now buy Mint Humbugs, Belgian Salt Liquorice and Sugar Sour Fizzballs by pressing a few buttons on your computer. The store uses Royal Mail in the UK for deliveries and Fedex for overseas orders.

Questions

1. What steps might The Oldest Sweet Shop in England take to offset criticism that they add to the volume of packaging and create environmental damage. *(You may wish to consider job creation and recycling when answering this question.)*

2. How might The Oldest Sweet Shop in England use the marketing mix to promote their online business?

3. Which of the many aspects of ethical trading might be described as simply good business practice? What kinds of business practice might you regard as being unethical?

Supplier relationships

Retailer purchasing power

Big businesses have market power. They rely on suppliers to provide their inputs but very often these suppliers are relatively small businesses, and their big customer is vitally important to their survival. Supermarkets like to be able to cut their prices, as this can increase their market share. But this may mean paring down the supplier companies' profits to an absolute minimum. The resulting competition can be tough for smaller businesses to live with.

On top of paying low prices, big businesses can squeeze their suppliers in other ways. They may want to raise quality standards without raising the price they pay. Or they may insist on paying invoices 30 or 60 days past the delivery date. The suppliers have to find the funds to give them trade credit. This can be extremely difficult for a small business.

In fairness, many businesses are now operating more efficiently than they would have in the past, and customers have benefited. Nevertheless, the business climate can be very harsh for SMEs (small and medium-sized enterprises). Some businesses strive for good relationships with their suppliers. But there are issues.

Products come and products go

It isn't really surprising that as time goes by, we see products both appearing and disappearing. Sometimes we are unaware of the many products and brands that have been around for some time and then disappear because there is something else in their place. We may regret the process of dismantling of such iconic names as Woolworths but did you notice the decline of Blockbuster, fighting a losing battle to survive where they once controlled the DVD market?

Recent TV programmes have told us about the 100 best musicals, the 100 best comedy moments and even the 100 top brands. We get daily news about the 'footsie', the Financial Times 100 Share Index, another 100 best. Amongst these, brands such as Marks & Spencer, Cadbury and Rolls Royce command instant recognition.

Newspaper columnists and internet bloggers tell us about the 'ones to watch' and, sometimes about companies that are 'doomed to fail'. The web site msnbc.com, which provides online news, reckons that 2012 will see the disappearance of such brands as Sears, Sony Pictures, Nokia, Saab, Sony Ericcson, My Space and Kellog's Corn Pops. Either they will be absorbed by other businesses or disappear altogether because they are no longer viable.

Questions

1. Habitat, Allied Carpets, Setanta Sports, Focus DIY, Waterford/Wedgewood, Dolcis, Kwik Save, Railtrack and Daewoo no longer exist. Which of these did you know about?

2. For each company you know about, give as many reasons as you can for their disappearance.

Product life Many products that have had long lives have gone. Pontiac, a major American car brand, has been shut down by struggling General Motors. Production of the Rover 75 ended when Rover came to the end of the road. The design of the Rover 75 was bought and adapted by the Shanghai Automotive Industry Corporation. Which brands have stood the test of time? We wouldn't be surprised to see Cadbury's on that list, or Coca Cola or Burger King. But given the relatively short life of the internet, would we include Amazon (set up in 1994, selling since 1995)? Google started in 1998, becoming the most popular website in the history of the internet. Should Google be included, and how about ebay, the online auction site, or Ask Jeeves (repackaged as Ask.com in 2005)?

Responding to demand

We saw in Section 1 how important it is for businesses to be market oriented. To survive, businesses have to look very carefully at their product designs. Customer tastes and consumer trends change at a frightening pace, influenced by many different things. Businesses must adapt their products and introduce new ones to meet these ever changing demands. This applies just as much to service providers such as retailers and fast food outlets as it does to manufacturers. Being market oriented is vital.

NPD

NPD

Adapting to change

On their web site, Cadbury describe the process of adaptation to customer requirements by saying:

"Product development is about designing and developing new products and modifying or upgrading existing products."

Product development at Cadbury involves the following stages:

- The initial idea
- The design of the product
- Choosing ingredients
- Creating prototypes, testing and testing again
- Costings, budgets – what plant and machinery do we need to make the new product?
- Choosing suppliers
- Production
- Finally – product launch

Not all new product ideas will go through all stages. At any stage, the product may be dropped or the idea changed.

Source: Adapted from www.skillsspace.co.uk/business_studies/16to19product_development

Cadbury launched its Dairy Milk bars in 1905 and they still sell well. In contrast, they launched Heroes in 1999. Heroes were designed to have an informal appeal, with a younger generation in mind. This was Cadbury's most successful innovation since the introduction of 'Roses' in 1938.

Questions

1. Why does Cadbury regularly develop new products, even though its older ones still sell well?

2. Why would Cadbury take so much care in the design of a new product?

Some firms lose track of what the consumer needs, either by not keeping a close enough eye on the market and failing to adapt, or because something completely new blows the rest of the market out of the water. If the business does not then adapt quickly it will have to discontinue the product and maybe close down.

Operations management

You can see from Cadbury's list of stages that developing a product involves a complex sequence of management decisions. Operations management is an umbrella term for all the processes that take the product from conception to sale.

- Design – where all aspects of the product are defined, so that it can be carefully positioned. The product must fill a gap in the market where it can compete successfully. The more closely it fits customer requirements, the better it will sell. Product design must draw on the best available technologies, provided the choice of technology is consistent with realistic pricing.

- Planning production – which means finding the most efficient and cost-effective way of creating the product. This involves identifying all the necessary inputs – the kinds of people who will be needed, the capital equipment, the finance and the most appropriate technologies.

Outsourcing

- Deciding on suppliers that might for example provide raw materials, equipment or components, advertising or distribution services. Some of these may be provided 'in house', by different departments of the business. But in some cases it will be more efficient to buy them from independent suppliers. It may make sense to outsource the entire production process: some businesses arrange for their products to be manufactured overseas, where labour costs will be lower.

In taking all of these decisions, businesses will have to choose the most appropriate technologies and have a clear view of how they will ensure that the product is of the quality that customers are expecting.

> **Operations management** refers to the many decisions that businesses must take about the entire production process. These are taken at every level in the business. Some will concern small scale, practical issues while others go to the heart of the firm's objectives.
>
> **Outsourcing** means buying in from independent suppliers rather than creating an input or product within the business. It can refer to a component part of the product or the finished product itself. Both manufacturers and service providers may outsource some of their functions.

The rest of this chapter and later ones will examine all aspects of the production process and show how businesses aim to produce competitively and profitably.

Planning production

The Design Mix – combining function, aesthetics and economic manufacture

A successful television programme (in terms of viewer figures), Grand Designs follows people building their own homes. In most of these programmes the houses built are large and go over budget. Nevertheless they attempt to combine function, i.e. a place to live comfortably; **aesthetics** – this may be a matter of taste but there is no denying the beauty of a lot of the projects; and **economic manufacture**. It is this last piece of the jigsaw that ultimately and perhaps inevitably proves the most difficult to achieve. (See Figure 7 opposite.)

Economic manufacture

Economic manufacture broadly refers to making, or in this case building, something that stays within budget, that is not wasteful and that would be competitive in its costing. The proof of the pudding concerning houses of grand design is difficult to measure as many of the houses will not be put up for sale.

> **Aesthetic** refers to perceived beauty, a sense that something is pleasing to the eye.
>
> **Economic manufacture** often involves producing at minimum cost whilst retaining the qualities that buyers are looking for.
>
> The **design mix** integrates all aspects of development so that the product can satisfy all likely customer requirements.

Achieving economic manufacture is often easiest when it is possible to mass manufacture. If very high output is unrealistic, it may help to use **batch production**. For example house builders will often prefer to build an estate of houses; in that way they can achieve economies of scale in purchasing, marketing, finance and managerial areas. They will pay less for their inputs and can spread advertising costs across a number of houses. But strategies for economic manufacture don't necessarily sit comfortably with a product that is aesthetically pleasing.

> **Batch production** is a method of production involving completing one operation at a time on all units before performing the next. This saves time.

Aesthetics

Aesthetics can be defined as an appreciation of beauty. Given that what is beautiful to one person may not be to another, an argument as to what is aesthetically pleasing may be a long one. Fans of minimalism in interior design may find that a lack of clutter is aesthetically pleasing; those who yearn for retro furniture may view that style as more aesthetic. The designer of a particular product will have a clear view of the aesthetics of their product but another designer may disagree. James Dyson's bladeless fan may be deemed aesthetically pleasing but its high price might suggest that it isn't economically manufactured.

The bladeless fan

Any newly designed product is going to incur research and development costs – in the case of Dyson's bladeless fan the design process evolved over four years. When Sir James Dyson first sought finance for his bagless vacuum cleaner none of the big banks would lend him money, presumably because they thought the project too risky or lacked the potential for profit. High pricing of such products may be a concern to potential lenders but necessary to recoup capital expenditure.

Dyson would probably argue that he was targeting 'early adopters'. His product didn't need to be economically manufactured because neither its unit cost nor its price needed to be as low as that of a standard fan. People who liked the concept and the aesthetic appeal of the bladeless fan might pay more for it anyway. Early sales suggest that he was right.

Questions

1. The bladeless fan sold well to the 'early adopters'. As sales increased, what would you expect Dyson to do?

2. What other examples can you think of, where the early adopters bought at a relatively high price? What happened to the price over time?

The design mix

Function

There is a presumption among buyers that a good is fit for purpose, i.e. that it fulfils the criteria of 'function'. This is an area that shouldn't be overlooked as a product's reputation is built on its ability to do what it sets out to do. This can be crucial to its success, more so than whether it is aesthetically pleasing or economically manufactured.

Figure 7: The design mix triangle

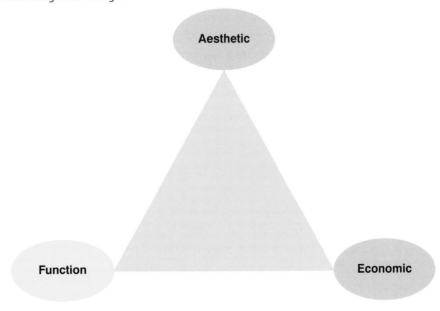

Show what you know

Try placing the following six products in the design mix triangle.

Example: a designer clothes item would probably fit close to the aesthetic tip of the triangle.

Product 1   Kettle   Product 2   Tag Heuer watch

Product 3   Push Chair   Product 4   Boots No 7 cosmetics

Product 5   Own brand cereal   Product 6   iPhone

Compare your answers with others in your group. Do not necessarily expect a consensus to emerge. For example would you place the iPhone closer to aesthetic than function?

Adapting to change

Timex and cost effectiveness

Consider the American firm Timex, a company that has been in existence in one form or another since 1854. At one time it had a major contract with the Disney Corporation to make Mickey Mouse watches and indeed today you can still buy a quality product, Mickey Mouse watch. But in the 1930s the watch was not so well made and the term 'a Mickey Mouse watch' was synonymous for cheapness and poor quality – clearly not something that Timex or any other brand would want.

After the Second World War Timex continued to produce affordable, durable mechanical watches for the mass market and became very successful. Then in the 1970s and 1980s the American watch and clock industry was devastated by the arrival of cheaper mechanical watches from the Far East as well as the development of digital quartz watches pioneered by Japanese companies. The worldwide Timex workforce of 30,000 fell to a core of just 6,000.

Instead of folding, Timex regrouped and rebranded as a quality product with a fashionable design, in particular moving into the sports watch market. The company sponsored many events, especially athletics. So successful was Timex that in 2001 the company was voted number one brand name in the U.S. Timex's three core vales are design, durability and performance.

Timex is a good example of a successful product that has stayed the same but has adapted to changing technology. The watches are more efficient and up-to-date. Undoubtedly Timex was slow to see the advent of competition from cheaper markets and from quartz watches. Perhaps they failed to spot the increasing material standard of living in many parts of the world, but they were able to regroup, re-brand and re-focus.

Questions

1. In 2008 Timex signed a four year deal to become the official timekeeper of the ING New York Marathon. What is the purpose of such deals?

   After the shock of losing market share to Japanese firms Timex increased its efforts on product quality. Longer battery life, more durable gold plating, greater accuracy and more water resistant styles were some of the improvements made. New quartz analogue movements were created, using fewer components and reducing overall production time and costs.

2. Explain why these changes were needed. How could these changes lead to greater efficiency in the future?

3. Was Timex's response to competition a change of product or a change in the way the product was made (product or process innovation)? Explain your answer carefully.

4. Timex has recently launched a range of fashion watches. Is this the way forward for the firm?

For discussion: Will watches become obsolete as iPhones and hand held computers render them unnecessary?

Chapter 7

Productivity and efficiency

Pyroban

Pyroban started life in Shoreham, Sussex in 1972 and has become a world leader in the design and manufacture of equipment for use in hazardous situations. They have a wide range of products, gas sensors and flameproof fork-lift trucks are just two examples. Customers include oil refineries, drilling rigs and mines. They are always trying to reduce costs and product development time. They have worked with engineering students at Brighton University to devise cost saving production strategies.

One student recommended investment in new software that links production equipment directly to the computer assisted design (CAD) system. Another student was able to speed up the product design process by using scientific rather than intuitive analysis of its markets and competitors. Both measures saved time and costs.

Both these developments involved process innovation – changing the ways they produce. But they are both also connected to product innovation – tailoring the product to the needs of the customer.

In 2011 the Pyroban Group was acquired by Caterpillar Inc. Want to know more? Just Google Pyroban.

Questions

1. Why is it important to save time and costs in these kinds of ways?

2. Pyroban is a manufacturing business. Would it be equally important to save time and costs in a service sector business?

3. How might McDonald's or Burger King set about increasing their efficiency?

Where do people work?

Economies can be divided into three sectors:

● The primary sector, agriculture, fisheries and forestry, and mining and quarrying – 3% of total production.

● The secondary sector – manufacturing, energy production and construction – 22% of total production.

● The tertiary sector – services – 75% of total production. This sector includes financial services, retailing, health, education, hotels and catering and public administration, among others.

Most people employed in the UK work in the tertiary sector. This is typical for a developed country. With the possible exception of Germany, many EU countries have seen their manufacturing sectors shrinking in recent years, as manufacturing activities were outsourced to countries with lower wage rates. In recent years, a new, fourth, sector has emerged, known as the quaternary sector and consisting of scientific research and development of new technologies. Pyroban fits quite well into this.

In a healthy economy there is strong competition. Effective businesses therefore strive to market better products that will cost less. Lower costs can mean higher profits or lower prices. Lower prices can mean higher sales, a larger market share or a loyal customer. Increasing **efficiency** and cutting costs go together. They are achieved when ways are found to produce with fewer resources.

In order to stay competitive, all businesses have to increase their efficiency. One way to measure efficiency is by looking at **productivity**, or output per person employed. On average, over time, productivity in the UK grows by just under 2% per year. New technologies and better ways of managing people are the main drivers.

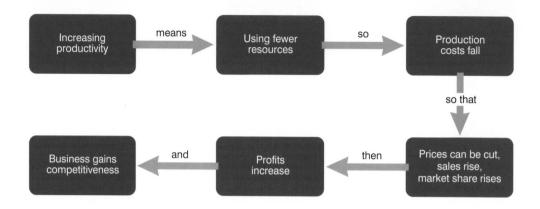

Efficiency means using resources in the most economical way possible. This means keeping costs to a minimum; businesses strive to organise their activities so that there is no wasting of employee time or of the capital equipment they use.

Productivity in the labour market is usually defined as output per person but a tighter definition is output per hour worked.

Labour or capital intensive?

The important ways of raising productivity are:

- Employing new technologies.
- Investing in more capital equipment.
- Training employees.
- Organising employees more effectively.

Notice that the first three of these involve up-front investment that can be quite expensive.

Almost all businesses will use a combination of labour and capital. The higher the wage rates that employers must pay, the more likely they are to use capital intensive production methods. Lower wage rates – e.g. in the Far East, will be associated with more **labour intensive** ways of producing. Typically, in the UK, as businesses strive for efficiency and low cost production, they tend to use more and better machinery and equipment, and fewer people. They become more **capital intensive**.

Capital intensive production uses a high proportion of capital equipment and a relatively low proportion of labour. It can cut costs in places where wage costs are high.

Labour intensive production uses relatively more labour, and works well where wages are generally low.

On the whole, capital intensity is likely to be found in the primary and secondary sectors. Service sector activities, by their nature, tend to be more labour intensive. However, even in health care, which is very labour intensive, the use of capital equipment is steadily increasing – think of scanners and heart monitors.

There is a problem with increasing productivity. Increasing capital intensity makes people more productive – helps them to produce more, faster. It makes it possible to pay them a higher wage and improves standards of living. But it also makes some of them redundant. For these people, standards of living may fall.

So people are often wary of capital intensive production. Yet without it, it is hard to raise standards of living.

Place the following statements into the category 'labour intensive' or capital intensive'.

- Production using extensive equipment and machinery.

- Requires a relatively high number of employees.

- Likely to be seen in job production (a method of production which employs all factors of production on one unit of production at a time, examples might be a wedding cake or a bespoke suit).

- Likely to be highly automated and produced on a large scale.

- Usually associated with large scale production of a standardised product, where each operation is performed continuously, usually on a production line (flow production, e.g. filling yoghurt pots or packing bags of sugar).

- More likely to be produced on a small scale.

Outsourcing

Competitive pressures

In the UK we have a guaranteed minimum wage but many countries do not, or their minimum wage is well below that of the UK's. This has led to many firms moving abroad or at least **outsourcing** their manufacturing needs to economies in the Far East and other places with relatively cheap labour. A business selling consumer goods which are traded for relatively low prices would find it difficult to compete if it manufactured in the UK. Rather than go out of business, firms move to producing abroad.

> **Outsourcing** means buying components or finished products from another business, rather than producing it 'in-house'.

A number of reasons have been put forward for the decline of the UK's manufacturing sector:

- problems with international competitiveness (high labour costs)

- limited investment in manufacturing

- unhelpful government policies, e.g. regulation

- trade union restrictive practices (fewer than in the past but still to be found)

- some changes in consumer demand may have been better catered for by foreign manufacturers, especially in the area of electronic consumer goods and in the car industry.

Dyson and others

Sir James Dyson believes that his firm would not be in existence if his products were made in the UK. He retains his research and development facilities in the UK but his manufacturing is carried out in Malaysia.

Look for merchandise with made in Britain on it and you will be hard pushed to find it in textiles, electronics, toys and cars. Even Marks & Spencer have shifted the bulk of their manufacturing abroad. Hornby, the maker of model trains and Scalextric, now manufactures its products in China.

A spokesman for the Confederation of British Industry said "The UK will never again compete on cost alone in a world where so many cheap goods can be made more cheaply elsewhere." But he also stressed the importance of not letting the UK manufacturing sector decline altogether. The CBI and other industry bodies are hoping that the sector can be kept alive by developing more specialised high technology products.

(questions overleaf)

Questions

1. What is meant by outsourcing?

2. Why have firms such as Marks & Spencer moved manufacturing production abroad?

3. When pressure groups are quick to exploit what they see as unfair practices in manufacturing abroad should British firms continue to manufacture in the Far East?

UK competitiveness

A report in the *Sunday Times* in 2010 stated that one in seven British companies with manufacturing facilities abroad had repatriated to the UK in the past two years. They had gone overseas to cash in on the eastern promise of cheap labour and cheap freight but the move had failed to take off. There are several reasons for this.

- Some firms are coming back to the UK because of a problem with the quality of overseas manufacturing.
- The exchange rate has fallen in recent years, making UK exports relatively cheap, and imports dearer.
- Wage inflation in some countries, especially China, has made the UK a little more competitive.

However, manufacturing's share of Gross Domestic Product (GDP) has fallen from 22 per cent to 11 percent over a period of only ten years. Businesses that do continue to manufacture in the UK may have to address skill shortages in some areas of manufacturing. Firms that may consider investing in the UK, such as Honda, expect high productivity from their workers and are prepared to invest heavily in technology to get the balance between labour and capital right. The UK will not again see the level of labour intensity in the manufacturing sector than it once did but investment in capital projects may protect more jobs than it loses.

One of the main growth areas in the UK in recent years has been in food retailing with the big supermarkets opening more and more branches and squeezing the independents out. But even in this sector there is a move to employing fewer workers with self service check out points and a similar situation at the petrol pumps. All of this forces down costs and improves productivity and ultimately, profits. If supermarkets can sell more or even maintain sales with fewer employees then output per worker or sales per employee will increase and unit costs will decrease.

Financing problems

At the other end of the scale small new businesses find it hard to succeed. Financing difficulties remain a stumbling block for new businesses. Banks are more reluctant to lend than they were prior to the banking crises of 2007/08 and are placing tough conditions on those they do lend to. After a short period of free

Firms like Honda will expect high productivity from workers when investing in the UK.

banking, a firm finding that it runs its agreed overdraft close to the limit and beyond, will find its debt to the bank growing quickly as high interest rate charges start to bite, alongside service charges. It is little wonder that potential entrepreneurs look at alternative sources of finance.

The availability of finance, or the lack of it, also affects larger firms and companies. These firms may seek to invest retained profits, if available, but if they are intent on replacing some labour with machinery, they too may need to seek outside finance. They must also invest in suitable training for their existing or remaining workforce, in order to reap the benefit of capital investment.

Show what you know

1. If a UK business wanted to become more capital intensive and less labour intensive how would it ensure that the quality of its remaining labour force was good enough?

2. What impact would a reluctance of UK banks to lend have on the future of British manufacturing?

3. Explain two forms of finance (other than banks) that small, new businesses may use.

4. How could the government offer support to small and medium sized enterprises (SME's)?

5. If you have a part-time job, think carefully about how your productivity could be improved. What actions would you or your manager need to take?

Operating efficiently

Capacity utilisation

Can staff work more effectively? Can machinery run for longer? Any firm faced with increasing demand for its products may need to consider these factors. Capacity utilisation looks at how much of the production capacity of the business is actually being used. It is a measure of efficiency and a key factor if the business wants to expand output.

$$\text{Capacity Utilisation} = \frac{\text{Current output}}{\text{Maximum possible output}} \times 100$$

This formula compares actual output with the potential output at full capacity. If is often said that a business should aim to operate at about 90 per cent capacity, on the grounds that unexpected orders can still be catered for. This measure can be misleading. Airlines with 100 seats on their planes wouldn't turn passengers away simply because 90 seats had been sold. Similarly a theatre with a 1,000 seat capacity wouldn't be content with 900 customers. It may be satisfied with a 90 per cent occupancy rate but it will strive to sell the remaining seats.

> **Capacity utilisation** measures actual output as a percentage of maximum potential output, per period of time.

In manufacturing the concept of full capacity may be queried. If a business operates from 8am to 4pm with all its machines in use all the time, it could be argued that it is operating at maximum capacity. The machines may then be cleaned and maintained for another hour. But why not operate two shifts of 8 or 12 hours, allowing a maintenance period in between the two shifts? If demand for the product is there, this approach would be cheaper than purchasing new machines. The cost of the capital equipment could be spread across a larger quantity produced.

Decisions like this might be part of an overall business growth strategy. Besides increased capacity utilisation, this might include:

● a bigger marketing effort, to create demand

● improved quality to increase market share

● careful attention to staff and customer needs, so as to retain both.

Increasing capacity

Weeks Trailers

This company made agricultural trailers for the farming community in the 1960s and 1970s. The firm evolved from very humble beginnings. One of the two brothers who started the firm was asked, by a workmate, to make a towing box to fit on to the back of a bike as a Christmas present for the co-worker's daughter. On production of this an order followed for a pram. The quality of the products was such that other orders quickly followed and the brothers opened a workshop in Hull to meet the demand.

One day a friend asked if they could make a trailer for the back of a tractor. Again the quality was good and word got round and further orders followed. Their premises were adequate and the existing staff were fully occupied. Their capacity utilisation was high. Out of the blue an enquiry from the Coventry based firm Massey Ferguson created an enormous problem for the brothers, Fred and Harry. To fulfil the order they would have to double their output. Even with an extra shift this would have been impossible in the existing premises – trailers take up a lot of space.

They had recently added hydraulics to their trailers and demand locally was increasing. They decided to buy larger premises which were purpose built. At the old premises steel was delivered to the front door but had to be moved to the far end of the factory where the cutting machine was situated. In the new factory a large entrance was organised so that lorries could disgorge their load of steel at the point where it was first needed. This improved the productivity of the firm; at a stroke more operations could be carried out in the same period as before, without production staff having to work any harder. The better layout created more space for storage and capacity could be increased leaving a better chance of fulfilling even more orders.

Massey Ferguson's trailers accounted for half the order and one of the brothers, Fred Weeks found lucrative markets in Africa. I worked at his company for two years and as I was leaving the company went public. Sadly Fred Weeks died not long after this and the business never fulfilled its huge potential. It closed down some years later.

Questions

1. Explain the terms under- and over-utilisation of capacity

2. What problems would have faced Fred and Harry Weeks when they had to decide whether to move to bigger premises? *(In answering this question consider, among other things, degree of control, suitability of premises, problems of existing workers when moving, finance and optimum size.)*

3. Weeks Trailers changed the layout of their factory in order to improve productivity and capacity utilisation. What other possible steps might they have considered to improve capacity utilisation?

A decision to purchase new machines is clearly a major one and is to be undertaken only after careful research into the nature of any possible increased demand. Equally so, a decision to implement an extra shift demands careful consideration. Where is the new labour to come from? How much training will be needed and provided for new workers? If it is 'on the job training', will this slow down the production process? If it is 'off the job' training, how much will it cost? Will there be increased wastage rates? At what capacity will the two shifts now run? Will machines last as long if used around the clock?

None of the questions posed above can be answered easily. Firms seeking to increase capacity may need bigger premises. This is why it is important for firms to carry out their research properly. A firm that is operating at 50% capacity has room for expansion but if the capacity utilisation is increasing, that rate may soon go higher. It may be possible to ask existing staff to work longer but they will probably need to be paid extra. Will the quality of what they produce in those extra hours be as good as in the normal shift hours? When these questions arise, the answers depend on the precise situation that the business is in.

Chapter 8

Stock control and just-in-time

Holding stocks

Stock control at Gadgets Ltd

Gadgets makes component parts for commercial vehicles. It tries hard to ensure that it always has adequate stocks of nuts and bolts. It has to carry more stocks than it usually needs, just in case it gets an unexpectedly large order.

The maximum stock that Gadgets can accommodate is 600 boxes. The company re-orders when stocks are down to 300 boxes. Normally the company needs about 120 boxes per week, but occasionally a big order comes in, requiring about 50 extra boxes. Orders are delivered about 8 working days after the order is received; this is known as the lead time. So it is important to have extra stock readily available in order to be able to fulfil all orders quickly.

Holding these stocks costs about £1,000 per month – they require warehouse space and they also have to be paid for, which means paying interest on the overdraft needed to cover this cost. Figure 8 shows how the stock control works in a normal three month period. It uses the idea of a buffer stock. This is the quantity of stock which is kept for emergencies, a stock that the business doesn't normally use.

Figure 8: Stock control

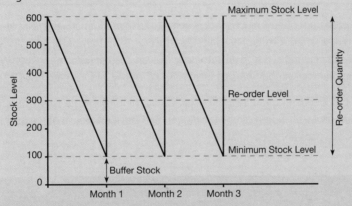

Questions

1. Explain why it is important to have a buffer stock.

2. Give three reasons why holding stocks may be costly.

3. Why might a shorter lead time when ordering stock be helpful to the business?

How much stock?

A manufacturing business may hold stocks of raw materials and components, of work in progress or of finished products. Managing stocks is an important part of running the business. In smaller firms the process of visiting a stock room to pick up parts and raw materials may still prevail. Conducting accurate and up-to-date audits of what they do and do not have in stock is important. Many businesses will have computerised systems to help them do this but others, particularly smaller firms, may use manual checks and written records. Some may rely on guestimates!

Very small firms may not keep any stock, if each order received requires different inputs. Then it is important to know how quickly a part or item can be obtained. A handyman who completes jobs in painting, decorating, electrics and plumbing would be brave or foolish to keep a stock of paint, light fittings and bathroom taps. It is impossible to predict demand in this case, and the cash that would be tied up in stock and storage facilities could be saved or used for other things.

Buffer stocks

Stock control diagrams

The **stock control** system must deliver materials and parts as they are needed in the production process if everyone is to be kept working efficiently. Figure 8 shows how **buffer stocks** work. This is a quantity of stock held back for emergencies, so as to ensure that production will not be held up if demand for the product is higher than normal, or the item is in short supply.

The stock control method shown in Figure 8 is called The Fixed Reorder Stock System. Stock is ordered at a fixed level (in this case 300 units) and usually at a fixed point in time, so that goods are delivered just before the stock levels reach the minimum level, in this case 100 units, i.e. the buffer stock level. When the lead time is known in advance, and is reliable, the system works. An order (in this case for 500 units) is made half way through the month. Even if the order takes two weeks to arrive there is more than enough stock to keep production going until the order arrives. This system operates well when everything runs smoothly but business, like life, has a habit of throwing up problems, hence the need for a buffer stock.

> **Stock control** is the process by which the business ensures that stocks of inputs are adequate to meet production requirements, and that stocks of the finished product are readily available to meet customer needs. At the same time, the cost of holding stocks must be kept down by avoiding holding more than necessary.
>
> **Buffer stocks** are kept to ensure that the business never completely runs out of either inputs or finished products.

IT systems keep track of how much stock is being used in production, and sales levels for finished products. In larger businesses, stock control and logistics (the process of transporting stocks to where they are needed) will be entirely computerised with an automatic delivery system for components. With good, easily accessed information, there are various ways of increasing efficiency and keeping down the cost of holding stocks.

● Quality products and good customer service can help to ensure that the business maintains a good reputation. Word-of-mouth can be the biggest and cheapest way to get regular business, and ensure that unsold stock does not accumulate.

Stock control includes making sure that stocks of finished products are readily available to meet customer needs.

Stock control matters

- Paying suppliers on time gets a business a good reputation. Not only this, but the firm may be able to get items at short notice and on discounted terms. This can help when orders or sales increase unexpectedly.

- Businesses that deal in products that are perishable or may deteriorate over time will be particularly careful about stock control.

- A build-up of stocks due to slow sales will be quickly recognised and orders can be cut to avoid holding unnecessary stocks.

Show what you know

The system of fixed re-order points and buffer stock levels are less commonly used nowadays, but they do give us an indication of how quickly stock levels can change and why buffer stocks can still be useful. Answer the questions below, using the data in Figure 9.

Figure 9

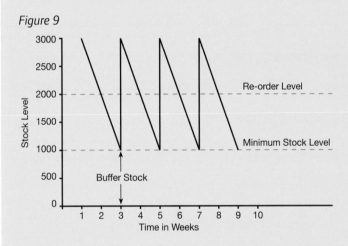

1. Work out what the re-order quantity is.

2. How long would the buffer stock last if a delivery was delayed?

3. Buffer stock represents unnecessary stock wastage – discuss.

Cutting costs

Just-in-time

During the period 1948 to 1975, Eiji Toyoda and his colleagues slowly developed a new approach to stock control called **just-in-time** or the Toyota Production System. The team saw that new methods of stock control could be an excellent way to increase efficiency and cut production costs. Their system is not simple and it does not work for all businesses. But since it was widely adopted in the 1980s and 90s it has transformed manufacturing processes in many countries including the UK. It is often useful for service sector businesses as well.

Just-in-time production keeps the cost of holding stocks to a minimum by planning production so that raw materials, components and work in progress are delivered daily or more often to the point where they are needed, at the appropriate time.

Just-in-time (JIT) stock control provides material, parts and accessories immediately prior to when they are needed, sometimes daily. The system either doesn't use buffer stocks at all, or reduces them dramatically. The delivery system allows firms to have smaller storage areas and hence lower insurance costs as less stock is held. The chance of stock being stolen or being lost is reduced, as is the problem of holding obsolete stock. Fewer people will be needed to administer stock control. This frees up working capital. Figure 10 shows how it works. Notice that there is no buffer stock.

Figure 10: Just-in-time stock control

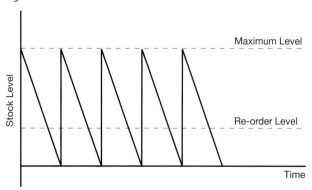

When JIT works well

How JIT works

Just arranging smaller but more frequent deliveries is not enough. For JIT stock control to work well there are several key requirements:

● Establishing good relationships with suppliers is paramount. Good relationships help ensure that stock arrives on time, and that the order is accurate. Suppliers need to be involved from the start, usually at the product development stage.

● The supplier must have a zero defects policy, which is essential to ensure that stock of the right quality is delivered. Often, the customer business and the supplier will work together to solve problems.

● Staff will need to be multi-skilled so that they can deal with problems as they arise.

● The IT system must be well designed and closely aligned to the needs of that specific business.

When the system is working well, JIT has many advantages. The biggest one is the cost saving – expensive warehousing facilities can be dispensed with. There is no need to keep stocks of finished products – everything can be produced to order. The business can respond quickly to orders and the product can be tailored to the specific requirements of the customer. This is known as a 'pull system' because customer demand pulls the production process.

JIT is a key element in lean production, which is covered in detail in Chapter 9.

What if something goes wrong?

There are disadvantages to JIT. The supplier relationship may prove to be excellent, but what happens when there is traffic congestion, or a breakdown, or worse still if the weather prevents delivery?

Have you ever been stuck in a traffic jam? Has a train you were due to travel on been delayed or cancelled? Has bad weather prevented you getting somewhere you desperately wanted to be? Did the snow of winter 2010 cause you any problems? Imagine those problems, applied to businesses relying on a just-in-time delivery. Time is lost; orders are not fulfilled; customer relationships falter.

The advantages of holding low levels of stock have to be weighed up against the disadvantages. Often there is no correct solution, only situations which sometimes are more suited to one particular approach, rather than another. Undoubtedly holding too much stock is unwise and not good business practice, but holding too little may cause just as many problems. Some businesses use JIT principles but do hold some stocks 'just in case'.

● If they order a little less frequently, they may be able to get better discounts from their suppliers.

● They may benefit from economies of scale if they make a batch of the products that have an assured market and then hold some in stock.

It will become clear that JIT operates well when everything runs smoothly but business, like life, has a habit of throwing up problems, hence the need for buffer stock in some situations.

Show what you know

1. Explain the problems that might arise if a business holds too much stock.

2. In what circumstances should a firm hold a buffer stock?

3. Evaluate the benefits and drawbacks of using a just-in-time stock delivery system for a large retail outlet.

4. Why is it important to get stock control systems in place in supermarkets?

5. Why might it be difficult to predict the level of stock needed in a business selling 'do-it-yourself' products?

Too much stock

Storing up trouble in board game land

In this world nothing is certain but death and taxes. So wrote Benjamin Franklin. Well, how about change? Only dinosaurs don't change with the times and we all know what happened to dinosaurs. And this can also be applied to business. A few years ago Sir John Harvey-Jones, a former CEO of a big chemical company, visited underperforming firms for a BBC TV show 'Troubleshooter', to point out problems and to suggest remedies. He was not short of examples to choose from.

Many firms find themselves with far too much stock and seem reluctant to do much about it. Many businesses feel that they must have stocks ready when and if demand for them arises. Some convenience food stores, for example, garner 90 per cent of their sales from 10 per cent of their 'lines', but continue to over-stock. A similar problem existed at a UK traditional board game manufacturer which had an annual turnover of over £2m, but was losing money. The company employed over 100 staff, had a large range of products for toy stores across the UK and Europe and produced many variants on their lines.

Each production line at this firm was efficient, well-organised, was run by only three people and had components close to hand. 40% of employees worked in production, 10% in administration, and 50% in the warehouse. You do not have to look very far to find out why the firm was operating at a loss. Stockholdings were running at £2.5m, with 5-10 per cent of this figure becoming obsolete each year. It took the warehouse staff longer to search for various stacks of boxes than it took to produce them. The owner was reluctant to change working practices.

The need to concentrate on about a dozen main products and palletize them was obvious. The owner was trying to concentrate on the many variations of products for customers and this was costing him money. The business needed a period of time to stop manufacturing, clear stock and start again by producing what the main customers wanted, when they wanted it. They needed JIT and lean manufacturing to enable them to cut costs, to survive and to become healthy. Sadly, the owner resisted change and the business failed.

Questions

1. State, in your own words, what the problem was at the board game manufacturer.

2. What is the problem with producing stocks of goods that have previously sold well?

3. How could JIT manufacturing have been used to help this manufacturer back into profit?

The board game company managers needed to adapt quickly and to adopt new strategies. They could have reduced stocks easily by applying the Boston Matrix to their product lines. Very often, in business, a range of approaches will be required to solve a problem.

Chapter 9

Lean management

Lean management, or lean production, at its simplest means minimising waste – waste of time and wasted resources. It tackles waste in a variety of ways. The point of adopting lean management techniques is to increase efficiency and develop a competitive advantage over rival firms. As a strategy, lean management includes:

- Careful control of stocks, both inputs and finished products, using JIT where appropriate.

- Attention to quality issues, reducing defects so that products are right first time.

- Continuous improvement – so that all members of the team contribute ideas about how to add value to the product or make the process of production more efficient.

- Reducing product development times so that the business responds more quickly to changing customer needs.

- Attention to training and developing employees' skills in other ways.

Chapter 10 concentrates on quality issues. Stock control and JIT were examined in Chapter 8. This chapter provides an overview of all aspects of lean production.

Tackling waste

Inefficiency

London: Police forces have wasted more than £500m over four years by assigning officers to back-office work, according to a report by Policy Exchange, a Conservative think-tank. Officers are employed in control-room and forensic-science posts that could be filled by support staff on lower pay. The report published in September 2011 stated that one in 20 officers were doing such work and that £147m a year had been wasted. The report argues that the planned 20 per cent cut in police funding over the next four years is manageable because of widespread inefficiencies that could be remedied. It costs £80,000 to train a police officer in ways of detecting and preventing crimes, dealing with suspects and collecting evidence. This training is not needed by the one in 20 employees identified in the report.

Beverley, East Yorkshire, 1970s: A road construction gang, due to start work on a road bridge over the River Hull arrive at work each day at 7.55am, for an 8am start and immediately put the kettle on. They start work at 8.15, break again for tea at 10.15am, for 15 minutes, and then work through until 12.30pm. Half an hour is taken for lunch and another tea break is taken at 2.30pm. They finish at 4pm. On Friday lunch times they have a 45 minute 'session' in the local pub. The contract is completed on time.

Questions

1. Identify areas of waste in the case of the construction workers.

2. The construction workers completed the contract on time. If their tea breaks had been shorter or were reduced in number, would the job have been completed earlier?

3. The report on the London police force identifies a number of police officers working in clerical posts. Is this a waste of resources?

4. In your opinion where should any money 'saved' by restructuring the police force be used? (Bear in mind that savings often equate to job losses.)

Lean management, lean production and lean manufacturing all refer to a wide range of strategies that can cut costs. Although these strategies were devised and implemented in manufacturing processes, many of them are also applicable in some service sector organisations. Successful lean management can eliminate bottlenecks and improve productivity by identifying procedures and product features that are non-essential.

The areas within which lean management has had a significant impact include:

- Just in time stock control and supplier relationships (see pages 43-47).
- Time based management in the production process – which could apply to the case studies.
- People management – which can emphasise flexibility, training and team work.
- Quality control.
- Product development lead times.

> **Lean management** encompasses a whole range of techniques for reducing waste and cutting the cost of production processes. These include product design and development lead times, quality issues, stock control (JIT) and the organisation of production.

As well as a reduction in cost and improvement in productivity arising from reduced waste, lean production provides the competitive advantages of better reputation, better quality, and better customer service.

Cutting costs

The manufacturing production process

Examples of waste in the production process include:

- time spent waiting for parts to arrive
- unsold stock having to be stored
- time wasted when the layout of a workplace is not conducive to efficient working, e.g. when there is too much movement of parts and labour around a factory
- money wasted when machinery is bought for a one off job then left lying idle
- people trained in a single skill will be idle when that skill is not required.

Firms should also consider whether they need their own transport fleets or whether money can be saved by hiring a logistics firm to carry out deliveries as and when necessary. The advantage of having your own lorry fleet and workers to drive them at any time of the day or night is often outweighed by the disadvantage of drivers and lorries' lying idle, and the payroll cost of employing the drivers.

The 'pull system', whereby finished products are created in response to customer orders, can be made to work efficiently by using **Kanban**. This is a system of cards used to trigger the movement or production of goods. In most car manufacturers, each car and each box of components will have its own Kanban card, which will carry instructions to move within the production process. So each vehicle can be tracked as it works its way through production. In many businesses Kanban is part of a sophisticated electronic system, which needs to be carefully organised in consultation with suppliers. It contrasts with mass production, where a large quantity of identical products were made and then held in stock to await orders.

Multi-skilling

Flexibility is also very important in lean management. This may apply to people – if they are multi-skilled, they can be kept busy in a variety of ways, attending to a range of production processes and moving to whichever of these needs most help. But it can also apply to capital. Machines that have only one use will be idle when not needed. Machines that can be programmed to make a variety of products can be used to meet changing customer choices. This is called **flexible specialisation**.

> **Time-based management** focuses on flexibility because this is the best way to avoid wasting time, either through some employees having nothing to do or some machinery idle. Short production runs meeting specific customer needs, together with flexibility, can cut the time taken in production. This approach fits neatly with JIT and Kanban.

> **Kanban** is a Japanese JIT system which uses cards to track stocks of inputs automatically, so that components are delivered to the right place at the right time. The system helps to co-ordinate production in the least wasteful way. Stock is pulled into the production process as it is needed. It requires very close relationships with suppliers.
>
> **Flexible specialisation** ensures that the business can change its products very quickly in response to changes in the market and customer demand. Both employees and machines can adapt to changing customer requirements.

Organising production

People management

Businesses look to eliminate waste by ensuring that tasks are carried out in the most efficient way. Some jobs, such as drilling holes in sheets of metal or packing first aid items into boxes are mind-numbingly boring, and workers may be encouraged, through the use of suggestion boxes or in discussion, to identify better ways of doing things.

Lean people management will often require multiskilling – ensuring that everyone is flexible and trained to carry out a range of tasks. This can help to give employees a greater sense of involvement in the production process. Encouraging them to spend time discussing ways of adding value to the product, or of saving time and cutting costs, is also an important element in lean management. Financial rewards are provided for all suggestions acted upon.

Quality

Defective products are a major source of waste, so it follows that reducing defects is key to lean management. Businesses can employ a zero defects policy. This means getting everything 'right first time'. This will have to include supplier businesses, and highlights the importance of good, close supplier relationships. It also highlights lean people management. Quality issues are examined in more detail in the next chapter. The case study below shows how quality may affect competitiveness.

Bangalore, India, August 2011

An American man, with a complex medical history, is having open heart surgery. The surgeon operates with robotic precision and calm professionalism. The patient had found out beforehand that these doctors perform significantly better than most Western hospitals and patients are five times less likely to suffer from post surgical complications than in the National Health Service (NHS).

The Indian hospital specialises in heart surgery. In 2008 its 42 surgeons performed more than 8,000 operations. As volume and quality increase, costs per operation come down. India has huge health problems, but is also a laboratory for a new generation of medical innovators. Aravind Eye Hospital in Tamil Nadu does 60 per cent of the NHS volume of cataract surgery at 1 per cent of the cost, yet its results are better than those of the NHS.

It has been argued that the NHS needs to close down 'under-performing' hospitals so that operations can be concentrated in centres of excellence. These proposals have met with stiff resistance. For example Leeds General Infirmary, which specialises in cardiac surgery for children, is one of those hospitals earmarked for closure with operations moved to Newcastle some 100 miles away. Yet Leeds has over three times more potential patients within a one hour drive than Newcastle.

Dr Phil Hammond, a General Practitioner (GP) suggests that the NHS needs to concentrate on:

1. An unwavering focus on performance.
2. Making doctors accountable for how money is spent, including design of hospitals
3. Finding ways for healthcare specialists to learn from other industries, aiming to make product defects so rare that they are a one-in-a-million occurrence.
4. Opening the NHS to competition.

All these suggestions have contentious elements, but any government in the UK must seek to get more from its health care system, not least because we are all living longer and will need more of the NHS's care in future. The NHS is consuming ever more of the nation's resources.

The authors were at pains to state that their study was not conclusive and that further investigation was needed.

Questions

1. Assess the arguments for and against having fewer centres of clinical excellence in the UK health service.

2. How might specialising reduce waste in a hospital context?

3. How might reducing defects benefit the hospital and the patients?

4. Can you identify any attempts to restructure your educational establishment so that it may reduce waste?

Beating the competition

Competitive advantage and short product development lead time

The concept of lead time was addressed briefly in a previous chapter. There are a number of definitions of product lead time, for example:

● The delay between initiation and execution of a process – a general use of the term.

● The period between a customer's order and the delivery of a final product. (This can relate to supplies of inputs or finished products.)

● The period between beginning and the completion of a production run.

This last use of the term 'lead time' can also relate to product development. This has become increasingly important: changing customer perceptions, demand for quality and new technologies have led to shorter product life cycles. This requires firms to have short product development lead times, while keeping production costs low and quality high, in order to stay competitive. A sustainable competitive advantage results from developing a superior product, and doing it quickly.

Competitive advantage is the advantage a firm gets over its competitors by offering customers greater value, either by charging lower prices, because their costs are lower or, adding value that provides better service and justifies charging higher prices.

Product development lead time refers to the length of time between the first emergence of the product concept and its launch into the market.

A short product development lead time can create a first mover advantage. The firm will be first into the market and can enjoy super-normal profits (exceptional profits) until other firms are attracted to the market and catch up.

Ways of shortening product development lead time include:

● Simultaneous engineering – making sure that different departments tackle different aspects of the development process at the same time, rather than one after the other. Teams can be working on design, engineering and marketing features of the product. If communications are good this can cut the development time and promote constructive discussion of any problems.

● Time based management – shorter production runs make it possible to update the product frequently. Flexible capital and training for multi-skilling will make the business much more adaptable when change is needed.

Give examples of three businesses that have benefited from shorter product development lead times, and explain why you selected each one.

Dealing with defects

Vehicles and defects

A study at Cambridge University in 2004, entitled Motor Vehicle Recalls: Trends, patterns and emerging issues, by Hilary Bates, Matthew Holweg, Nick Oliver, and Michael Lewis, looked at the increasing number of vehicle recalls in the UK over a period of time and tried to find reasons for this.

The study found that more than one million vehicles had been recalled in each of the previous five years in the UK. Some of these were vehicles that had been recalled more than once. It may be that manufacturers are more fearful of litigation than they used to be and that this has increased the likelihood of recall, even though there are no more faults with their vehicles now than there were years before.

We know that product development lead times in the automotive industry have been falling. Is one of the side effects of faster times-to-market that the vehicles have more faults when they get to markets?

According to the study, East Asian producers represent 8 out of the best 10 companies with the lowest recall rates. Not for them the problem of unusual acceleration, or brake failure – or at least not during the period of this study. In the study Toyota was able to enjoy simultaneously low recall rates, high product variety and short product development lead times, where others didn't. (In more recent times it would appear that Toyota, too, have 'taken their eye off the ball'.)

In an attempt to drive down costs, most automotive manufacturers are trying to squeeze more out of a reduced number of platforms, i.e. they are using the same platform for an increased number of models. Maybe increased recalls are a consequence of this?

Questions

1. What is meant by the concept 'short product development lead time?

2. Identify and explain one advantage to a manufacturer of a short product development lead time.

3. Analyse the use of short product development lead times for manufacturers in gaining a competitive advantage over their rivals.

4. Evaluate the potential advantages to car manufacturers of having shortened product development lead times against the drawbacks of an increasing number of product recalls.

Find out more

The Japanese car firm Toyota has adopted this philosophy over a period of time. Investigate Toyota's research into the 7 principles of Toyota Production and Toyota's 14 management principles. (There is also a Toyota six rule system associated with Kanban and additional information is readily available.)

Quality in the food industry

Food safety is vital in all areas of the industry. There have been a number of instances of firms going out of business when their food quality has been found to be defective. Discoveries of bacteria in food get national news coverage, of both the event and the food supplier, and can ruin the latter's reputation.

To help reduce these instances a number of local authorities operate 'scores on the door' schemes where all establishments selling food have annual inspections and are graded either A to E or 1 to 5, depending on a number of factors relating to fitness for purpose.

At McDonald's the firm concentrates on five main ingredients in order to meet quality requirements – beef, chicken, bread, potatoes and milk. Relationships with suppliers are of particular importance for all those involved. McDonald's, like all food outlets, are subject to random inspections so it is important that all their outlets meet the required standards: a bad reputation at one outlet will damage all outlets.

Questions

1. Explain two reasons why quality matters greatly in food outlets.

2. What quality issues can you think of that would affect (a) manufacturers of cars and (b) clothing suppliers?

Competing on quality

Quality control

Traditional **quality control** in manufacturing involves inspecting and checking work that has been completed. Every product may be inspected, or a sample may be taken. Quality targets may be set, whereby the number of defective products must be kept below a certain percentage. This approach was suitable for assembly-line production where each person performs a single task. Employees might have few skills and little insight into the production process. Sometimes managers feared that rigorous quality control might raise costs and threaten profits. So this approach was not generally associated with high quality. You can see straight away that this kind of quality control would not work well at McDonald's.

When it became clear that UK products were often not competitive in global markets (in the 1980s), it was realised that competing producers were emphasising much higher levels of quality control. Lean production techniques were gradually being adopted and it was seen as wasteful to be producing faulty products.

> **Quality control** means, quite simply, ways of ensuring that quality is maintained. Traditional quality control means inspecting and checking for defects, and this has been superseded by the idea of quality assurance.

Nowadays, for large scale manufacturing such as vehicle production, simply inspecting and checking products would be risky, even if components and work in progress were checked before a final inspection. This approach is now seen as outdated in many industries. Its place has been taken by a whole raft of strategies that make quality an ever-present preoccupation for most businesses.

Quality assurance

High quality is now seen as an important component of added value, which gives the product value for money and a competitive advantage. Competition has driven up customer expectations. To meet these expectations, quality improving strategies have been developed. Many businesses have a zero-defects strategy – which means getting the product right first time.

Quality assurance

Strictly speaking, quality assurance involves having a well publicised system that documents the process by which quality is achieved. ISO 9000 is an example of this – it is an international procedure providing certificates that are designed to ensure that a quality system is in place. Other examples are set out in the case study below. Supplier businesses have to be involved in the certification too. But the term 'quality assurance' is also used much more loosely to refer to measures that can generally improve quality.

The search for better quality has been continuous. One way to improve it is to make all employees responsible for quality. Quality assurance entails a commitment to collaborations between design, production and marketing teams. They will work together to achieve quality and reliability. Instead of monitoring output as the old quality control departments did, a QA department will be drawn into the design process and the setting up of the production system. Customer requirements will be considered and high quality will be planned at every stage.

> **Quality assurance** takes into account customers' needs and involves businesses in examining every aspect of design, development, production and marketing. All employees will be aware of the need for attention to quality and there may be a zero-defects policy. Quality becomes part of the culture of the business – the attitudes, customs and expectations that influence the way decisions are made in that business. This approach to quality is just as relevant for the primary and the service sectors as it is for manufacturing.

Examples

The Quality Assurance Agency for Higher Education. Its job is to uphold quality standards in UK universities and colleges. It provides guidance and checks the quality of teaching and assessment in UK higher education, in order to give every student the best possible learning experience.

Visit Scotland's quality assurance scheme tells customers what to expect from the hotels, guest houses and restaurants belonging to its organisation. It enables businesses to benchmark themselves against other similar businesses. Based on customer research, each award is a thorough professional assessment reflecting the quality criteria that customers really value. Visitors are able to give customer ratings and these views drive the process forward.

Red tractor food

Following food scares and foot-and-mouth funeral pyres, British agriculture was forced into a fundamental rethink of the way food was produced, in order to restore confidence amongst consumers, processors, retailers and overseas buyers.

The resulting Red Tractor food assurance scheme has strict guidelines for food safety and hygiene, animal welfare and environmental protection. It is policed on 78,000 farms by independent inspectors and overseen by the Assured Foods Standards agency. Farmers now work to cut fuel, fertiliser, crop protection, animal medicine and irrigation water inputs, often using sophisticated computer systems and GPS guided equipment.

Farming minister Jim Paice says this gives 'Made in Britain' an incredibly powerful message to emerging markets.

Questions

1. How have the principles of quality assurance been applied in a) the farm sector and b) the service sector?

2. What links can you see between the developments in quality assurance and the approach of McDonald's to quality issues?

Customer consultation

There are several ways of ensuring that customers' views are taken into account. Customers may be consulted through market research, either before a product is manufactured or at the trial stage. They may be asked to join a consultation group involved in the design and manufacturing of the product. Clearly such invitees have to be knowledgeable about the product being considered. A firm that doesn't listen to its customers is a firm that will struggle. Firms should always take the views of their customers into account.

Comparisons of quality assurance with quality control are best made in manufacturing. The consensus view nowadays is that inspection at the end of a process, with the aim of finding faulty products and then throwing them away, is too late, ineffective and costly. Quality requires improvement of the production process. This is why quality control departments have generally become obsolete and inspection has been replaced by a process of continuous improvement that is carried out by those involved in the making of a product.

Continuous improvement

One way to improve quality is to embrace the idea of **continuous improvement** or **Kaizen**. This too is part and parcel of lean production. It is all about minimising waste and finding better ways of organising the production process. Kaizen is seen as involving continuous improvement in all walks of life, including social and home life.

Kaizen is an umbrella term that can include any aspect of productivity and specifically JIT, Kanban and zero defects. So it does have a part to play in quality improvement.

Quality circles

One way of encouraging continuous improvement in quality is to make use of **quality circles**. These are small groups of employees who can meet regularly and look closely at the way they might improve quality. Meetings should be chaired, even if informally. It is usual for a senior manager to be included in a group. Training should be provided.

After groups have held discussions they may make recommendations or present findings to management. Quality circles are often introduced as ways of motivating employees and they can help with the delegation of responsibility.

Figure 11: Quality circles

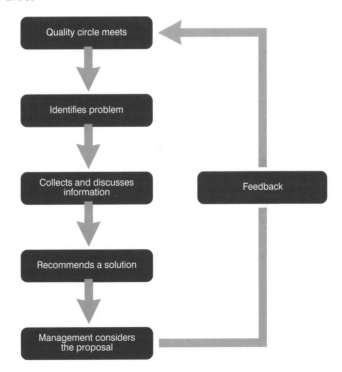

> **Kaizen** means continuous improvement in Japanese. It implies that the business will be constantly searching for new ideas about how to produce more efficiently. Usually these ideas will come from employees who are actually involved in the production process.
>
> A **quality circle** is a small group of employees in the same area of production who meet regularly to study and solve all types of production problems.

TQM and lean production

Total quality management (TQM)

TQM is a philosophy that fosters both an individual and a collective responsibility for quality at every level. It originated in Japan as part of the lean management developments. It was gradually adopted in other countries and became fashionable in the 1990s but is rather less referred to now. However, it dovetails well with quality assurance, Kaizen, zero defects and lean production generally as in theory, no product should proceed past the point where a fault has been identified.

With TQM, each department is seen as having responsibility for quality in both products and services. It is expected to regard the department handling the next stage of production as its customer, whose needs must be satisfied. With strong market orientation and attention to the final customer's expectations, this means that the impetus to provide quality and reliability runs right through the system. If problems are stopped before they occur rather than finding them after they occur, time is saved as well as money. The process of continual checking can be laborious and time consuming, but if carried out correctly, time is saved through having very few wasted products.

Quality assurance requires a change of culture and attitudes within the business. Even more so, TQM demands the involvement of the whole workforce and therefore requires a substantial investment in training and reorientation. This is costly but there are very few businesses that have not addressed quality issues in recent years. Increased competition and better informed customers have made action on quality essential.

> **Total quality management** involves getting all employees to focus on quality, so that every team or department sees the user of their particular product as a customer who must be satisfied. There must be a change of culture so that quality issues will be addressed by all. Quality circles and zero defects policies fit in well with this approach.

If adopted in full, TQM is a complex procedure and is not suited to every business. Towards the end of the 1990s, business experts reported that 93% of America's largest 500 firms had adopted it in some form. A claim that TQM can be implemented in any organisation – manufacturing, service, non profit or government is controversial. However, many businesses have adapted the TQM approach to suit their own circumstances, using the ideas that are most likely to be helpful and rejecting those that do not fit their circumstances.

Two points of view

For TQM

- TQM generates improved products and services, reduced costs, more satisfied customers and employees and ultimately better financial performance.

- Successful quality circles are likely to accept and adopt aspects of TQM, as they are given more responsibility to deal with demanding situations.

Against TQM

- There are significant costs of implementation; excessive retraining is required, as well as inordinate amounts of senior management time and there is increased paperwork and formality.

- Expectations about employee commitment levels are unrealistic.

- TQM fails to address the needs of small and service businesses.

The TQM package

The requirements of TQM

- **Committed leadership** – unwavering, long term commitment by top managers who adopt and promote TQM using mission statements, themes and slogans, with good communications at every level.

- **Employee empowerment** – greater employee involvement in design and planning, and greater autonomy in decision making.

- **Increased training** – includes TQM principles, team skills, problem solving.

- **Process improvement** – reduced waste and benchmarking – researching and observing best competitive practice.

- **Zero-defects mentality** – a system in place to spot defects as they occur, rather than through inspection, with constant performance measuring and monitoring.

- **Closer customer relationships** – determining customer requirements, and then meeting them no matter what it takes.

- **Closer supplier relationships** – working closely and cooperatively, often sourcing key components from just one supplier.

Show what you know

Wherever possible, give examples drawn from specific businesses that you know about.

1. Outline the basic differences between quality control and quality assurance.

2. In what circumstances might there still be a place for traditional quality control?

3. Why are the views of customers important when adopting quality assurance?

4. Are there greater difficulties involved in implementing TQM in a service organisation rather than in a manufacturing firm?

5. Examine the importance of Kaizen to the process of TQM.

6. Could TQM be implemented in small firms or is it for larger firms only?

Fridge freezers

Chris Parry wanted a new freezer for his garage, so he could store more of the special offers, BOGOF items and bulk orders of meat. The local electrical store sold him just what he wanted at a very reasonable price. He was careful to check that it would work in his garage.

After just one day, the new freezer stopped working. Chris contacted the supplier and they quickly installed a replacement in the garage. But the replacement failed too. Chris made enquiries with the manufacturers and found that the fridge freezer he had bought was unsuitable for a cold place. He spoke to the store manager and was advised to write to customer relations. They were unsympathetic.

Many emails later, the electrical store offered to repair the freezer. But Chris pointed out that it would never work in his garage in winter, that he had told the store at the outset that he would be putting it in the garage, and therefore it was not fit for purpose. He threatened legal action and eventually got a full refund.

Questions

1. Why is it important for customers to be protected in this way?

2. How might the store have avoided this situation?

3. How do you think businesses generally responded to consumer protection law?

Up to now, this section has focused on the management of production from the business point of view. This chapter concentrates on the rights of the consumer.

Has anyone in your family been persuaded to take out an endowment mortgage, without being warned that its value could in certain circumstances go down? In recent years UK banks have had to put hundreds of millions of pounds aside to help repay customers who were ripped off. This mis-selling occurred because they were given misleading quotes and insufficient information, not only about mortgages but also about payment protection insurance and other financial products.

The need for protection

Companies exist primarily to make profits to reward their shareholders. Enlightened companies may see that the best way to reward their shareholders is to please their customers by giving value for money in terms of price and service. Unfortunately not all businesses think that way. So governments legislate to protect the consumer from faulty goods and poor services. This protection has been built up gradually over many years. You do not need to have detailed knowledge of the many acts of parliament, if you are studying for Edexcel AS Business. But you do need a clear overview of consumer protection generally.

The law

Perhaps the most important consumer protection measure is the Sale of Goods Act 1994. This law requires that when a consumer buys an item from a trader, it must be:

● of satisfactory quality – free from defects

● fit for purpose – for the use for which it is intended

● as described – matching the description on the packaging or what the trader tells the buyer.

Chris, in the case study above, was using these legal requirements to fight for his rights. If an item doesn't comply with any one of these rights, it is faulty and the customer has the right to repair, replacement or refund. There are fewer rights if a good is bought from a private seller – items need only match the seller's description and be theirs to sell.

The Trade Descriptions Act of 1968 had a big impact on advertising. Until then, businesses routinely made claims in their adverts which exaggerated the good qualities of their products. The Act made it a criminal offence to give a false description of the product being sold.

> **Consumer protection** consists of a set of laws that make businesses accountable to their customers. Products must be fit for purpose and accurately described. Some aspects of consumer protection are resented by businesses because they raise costs.

Focus on quality

Consumer awareness has increased greatly through media coverage of poor standards in the business world. The Consumer Association (CA) in particular has exposed careless practice and poor design and a variety of activist groups have posted information on the internet. When they do not get satisfaction from their purchases, aggrieved customers can turn for advice and support to the CA, Citizen's Advice Bureau, the National Consumer Council and regional Trading Standards services.

Consumer protection legislation has forced businesses to place more emphasis on the quality of both goods and services that they supply. It has given added impetus to businesses to set up customer service departments, so that complaints can be properly dealt with before they become serious.

Show what you know

Look for two or three examples of consumer protection that have affected individuals – yourself or someone you know or have heard about. Explain what difference the legal requirements have made. Share at least one story with someone else in your group.

Energy prices

The electricity and gas industries in the UK are dominated by six big firms, who between them hold 99 per cent of the market share. They have real market power. Despite the fact that wholesale prices in the gas industry have risen and then fallen there is a widespread perception that the companies are quick to put up prices and slow to bring them down.

In the UK 'fuel poverty' has become an issue. Households where fuel bills account for more than 10 per cent of total spending are said to be in fuel poverty. This affects single people, low earners and pensioners in particular. In the UK the average household fuel bill in November 2010 was £1069 per annum. Nine months later it had risen to £1293, a rise of almost 21 per cent. Fuel prices have risen by 96 per cent in five years and now 6.9m people or 27 per cent of households are in fuel poverty in the UK (September 2011).

Questions

1. Think of as many reasons as you can why energy prices might have risen.

2. To what extent can people cut back on energy consumption?

3. What does your answer to question 2 tell you about the price elasticity of demand for energy?

4. To what extent, and in what ways, do you think that energy companies have taken advantage of customers?

Regulation

Because there are just six major energy companies that dominate the market, and because energy has a particularly crucial role in the economy, there is a **regulator** for the industry, OFGEM (the Office of Gas and Electricity Markets), which controls the extent to which gas and electricity prices can be raised. It monitors the value for money that customers can obtain. The difficulty is that energy prices are gradually rising, as energy becomes more expensive to deliver. For example, traditional gas sources are diminishing and new sources, e.g. shale gas, cost more. Worldwide, demand for energy is increasing over the long run, putting pressure on prices.

Competition law tries to ensure that firms do not fix prices by entering agreements with their competitors.

Regulators

Other utility regulators oversee the running of the phone systems (OFCOM), water suppliers (OFWAT), and other important parts of the infrastructure of the economy. Some of these regulators have been quite successful in preventing overcharging but there is often controversy surrounding their activities. In the case of energy, it is difficult to work out which of the competing suppliers might offer the best deal. This suggests that the energy companies are deliberately trying to avoid real competition by making their pricing systems as confusing as possible. (This pricing policy is sometimes referred to as confusion pricing.)

Businesses need to make profits, it is argued, so that they can re-invest and ensure long term supplies. But in some industries, price rises have led to substantial profits. The body that has responsibility for ensuring that there is genuine competition wherever possible is the **Office of Fair Trading** (OFT).

Regulators are independent bodies set up by the government for industries that had previously been nationalised and had had some monopoly power. These industries still have considerable market power because the infrastructure they provide cannot easily be replaced by competing systems. (Think of gas and water pipes.)

The **Office of Fair Trading** oversees UK competition policy. It investigates complaints about unfair competition and possible mergers that might reduce competition. It takes care of many aspects of consumer protection, including trade descriptions.

Unfair competition

Competition law

The Companies Act 1998 states that firms must not:

- fix prices, i.e. they must not agree prices with competitors
- limit production to reduce competition (and drive up prices)
- charge different prices to different customers (this part of the law is notoriously difficult to police as firms can offer all sorts of discounts)
- agree not to bid or tender for certain contracts – there have been examples of firms tacitly agreeing not to move into certain markets, so that several sellers can share the market without having to compete on price.

The OFT was established in 1973. It enforces competition law and prohibits abuse of a dominant market position. It operates under the supervision of the Director General of Fair Trading. The OFT is responsible for overseeing matters relating to consumer protection and aims to ensure that no business deliberately restricts competition.

Competition and customer care

Are OFT powers strong enough to maintain strong competition? Does the OFT implement the law with sufficient force? These are controversial questions. Recent investigations include the pricing of dental work; the price fixing of sales of hotel rooms via the internet; cartels in the commercial vehicle market, and the pricing of ebooks. There is clearly a need for a body such as the OFT as almost all of their investigations start as a result of a complaint. But many investigations take a long time; sometimes it is concluded that the companies concerned are largely blameless.

The full workload of the OFT gives an indication that the consumer does need protecting. The purpose of consumer legislation is threefold:

- To ensure that providers of goods and services clearly understand the legal requirements as to the customer care they must provide.

- To establish the procedures of redress for customers.

- To establish legal procedures for dealing with sellers who are in breach of the legal requirements.

Ripping the shirt off your back

In 2002, the OFT received a complaint about replica football shirts. The scandal centred on an apparently illegal agreement to inflate the price of Umbro shirts for Manchester United. Emboldened by new powers in the Competition Act 2000, OFT investigators launched a series of early morning raids and seized incriminating documents.

After a 14-month investigation, Manchester United, a leading sports kit manufacturer and eight retailers were found guilty of collusion, i.e. a secret agreement, to fix the prices of replica shirts. They were fined a total of £18.6m. The OFT said the severity of the fine reflected the scale of this national conspiracy to cheat consumers. Even the game's governing body, the Football Association, was found guilty of maintaining the price of England shirts by restricting supply through Britain's biggest sports retailer, JJB Sports.

Immediately following the ruling, the supermarket chain Asda cut the price of Manchester United shirts, now made by Nike, at 27 of its stores, by £15, to just under £25.

Questions

1. Why were the retailers willing to charge similar prices, instead of competing against each other?

2. Why is collusion illegal?

3. Explain the role of the Office of Fair Trading.

4. Given the number of investigations undertaken by the OFT, what conclusions can be drawn as regards the punishments meted out?

Find out more

Research and comment on an OFT investigation – start out at www.oft.gov.uk/news-and-updates/.

Running cafés

Kaye Walker owns and runs two cafés in Beverley, East Yorkshire. Until recently she was convinced that the market size was restricted to customers visiting the historic market town plus those who shopped or worked in Beverley. She was also constrained by the number of customers she could accommodate in her establishments. She had historical information on her previous sales levels.

Her market consists of customers who come to eat in her café or to take food away. She has a number of competitors in Beverley, including national chain outlets. She thinks that price is not an area in which she can gain a competitive advantage. Kaye feels that personal service, combined with a choice of fresh food, prepared on site, will be her USP. In the past she has tried to build up delivery of specialised products, e.g. pork pies and Christmas cakes and she has done some outside catering. But the market has been stagnant or even declining recently, as people are cutting back on eating out.

Kaye has thought about putting one of her two cafés on the market (to sell) but the economic climate deters possible buyers. She has decided to take a gamble by investing in a web site to bring her catering skills to a wider market – not an international one of course, although it is possible to sell food to overseas markets. Kaye hopes to attract firms and families throughout East Yorkshire who may need catering for functions, varying from funerals to fundraising, and from parties to presentations. She has employed a web designer and is exploring ways of getting early hits on browsing sites. Kaye has spare capacity in her production facilities and can cope with extra demand.

Questions

1. If Kaye cut her prices, how would her business be affected?

2. When Kaye introduces her web site she will need to prepare a sales forecast for the year. What difficulties may she face in preparing this forecast?

3. How could having a web site create a way to increase potential sales?

4. What other strategies would you advise Kaye to try in order to increase her sales?

5. How much of a risk is Kaye taking?

Risks

Businesses need to think ahead. They have to take decisions in the present but these decisions will have consequences. Risks arise when decisions have to be taken without knowing what is going to happen in the future. To reduce risk, businesses try to think about how their markets and their costs of production might change. There are many kinds of external influences that can alter the situation unexpectedly, but being aware of the possibilities will help.

In the case study, Kaye is hoping to enlarge her market by offering products further afield. She is paying for a web site without knowing whether customers will respond. If she needs to approach a bank for help with finance, the bank will want to see a business plan and this will have to contain an overall **forecast** for each aspect of the business. This will help the bank make a realistic assessment and more importantly, will provide a good guide for the business in its efforts to plan for the future.

Kaye's businesses are relatively small. She faces considerable uncertainty because she is trying to expand when the economy is in recession. Larger firms may have their own sales department and will be able to carry out their own market research. Some businesses will employ outside experts to carry out market research for them. This will make it easier to produce reasonably accurate sales forecasts. This in turn will help the business to plan for the future.

Forecasting

The level of sales that a firm will make in a period, usually a year, depends on:

- The market size.

- The market structure – where and who the potential customers are.

- The market share you can achieve, and the competition you face.

- The market trends – is the market growing or declining, or is it static?

- The investment in terms of time and money, needed to sell the product.

With so many unknowns to consider, forecasting is difficult. Future sales may be subject to changing fashions or new technological developments. Costs may depend on world market prices or skill shortages that make it difficult to recruit. But producing forecasts forces businesses to draw up plans.

> **Forecasts** involve estimating future sales revenues, costs and profits. They may involve some guesswork but this should be informed by the best available information, e.g. market research.

How can forecasting be made easier?

An old business saying goes like this: 'stick to its knitting'. In other words, businesses should concentrate on what they do best. For new and recently started businesses the firm should have a core activity to focus on. This will make forecasting that little bit easier.

Some businesses use historical data and extrapolate their forecasts from that. If sales revenue was £100,000 in year 1 and £150,000 in year 2, this would suggest that in year 3 it might be £200,000. Alternatively, it might be another 50% increase, taking it to £225,000. An outsider might think this was much too optimistic.

If the business is likely to be much affected by the state of the economy, then some understanding of economic trends will help in making realistic forecasts. For example, a dress shop selling high end fashion products might do rather badly in a recession and avoid expanding at a time when real incomes are falling.

Show what you know

How can forecasting help a business? Think of a business you know and imagine what plans it might have to increase sales. What kind of information would it need in order to produce reasonably accurate forecasts? What unknowns might make the decision difficult? When you have done this, compare your notes with someone else who has done the same.

External influences

Predicting future sales levels

The interpretation of past data is known as **time series** analysis. A business may look at past sales data for a period of ten years. If trading conditions have been stable this might not be too difficult. If short term trends are all that is needed this is not too difficult either. In order to get figures that are as accurate as possible, market researchers will need to look at trends or patterns. They will also need to study the cyclical fluctuations – change associated with the business cycle of boom, recession, depression and recovery.

Governments try to use fiscal policy (taxation and government spending) and monetary policy (predominantly interest rates) to keep the economy growing at a steady pace. There have been times when growth has been steady at around 2 per cent per year, but subsequently, the economy seems to have reverted to fluctuating growth rates. Knowing how the business is likely to be affected by these external influences is important. (See the case study overleaf.)

Businesses also need to study seasonal fluctuations, if they are likely to be affected by them. Businesses based on tourism, arable farms and greetings card producers all fall into this category. In addition, some swings in business demand will be random fluctuations, and as the name suggests these are almost impossible to predict.

Recession

Construction

Many people in the UK, where house ownership is relatively high compared to some other European countries, will have grown up believing that if you put your money into property you were 'on a winner'. If you bought a house in 2007, especially so if you were a first time buyer, this would not be the case. In 2008 the international banking crisis led among other things, to much less bank lending for house purchases. Furthermore, banks that in the past were prepared to lend more than 100 per cent of the value of a house, began to demand 25 per cent deposits.

A vicious circle ensued. House prices fell as potential buyers couldn't get mortgages and owners took their property off the market because they were not getting back the price they paid. (The technical term for this is negative equity, where the value of the house is less than the amount borrowed.) Builders were reluctant to build and there were huge knock-on effects for furniture businesses, sellers of carpets and ancillary products, and estate agents and firms selling decorating products. Four years later the market still hasn't recovered. This lack of growth leads to further knock on effects in the economy: those people who lose their jobs as a result of the recession cut back on their spending, particularly on luxury products.

Questions

1. What is the difference between cyclical fluctuations and seasonal fluctuations?

2. The fall in house prices in 2007/08 was directly related to the recession. For large established firms in the building industry, what difficulties might they face when trying to estimate sales during and after the current slump in demand?

3. Explain the effect of a fall in demand on the sales of (a) supermarkets, and (b) sellers of middle price-range cars. What difficulties would the manufacturers of such cars face in estimating their sales over a period of time?

4. Faced with falling demand for their products how might (a) manufacturers of furniture, and (b) retailers of furniture, try to increase demand?

Cash flow forecasting

Cash is the lifeblood of any business. It is not the same as profit (see Chapter 15). On paper a business could be making profit but if cash is not coming into the business, for whatever reason, then that business will not survive for long. Delays in receiving payment, worse still not receiving payment at all, make running a business almost impossible. Payments to creditors have to be delayed and if this happens on a regular basis then suppliers will stop supplying and the firm is on the slippery slope to failure. Employees may well lose confidence in their future prospects and leave as soon as they can find another job.

A **cash flow forecast** is a record of cash received by the business and expenses that have to be paid for. In a business plan, a cash flow forecast should be prepared for the minimum of a year, usually split into monthly or four-weekly periods. Looking at past cash flow calculations, a pattern may emerge and highlight long term trends or seasonal variations for which the business should be prepared.

> **Time series:** data that covers a period of time so that trends can be observed. These trends might reflect seasonal changes or changes in customer preferences or the business cycle.
>
> **Cash flow forecast:** a record of cash in from sales and cash going out in payment of costs. The difference between the two gives the net cash flow.

If the cash outflow is greater than the inflow, there is said to be a negative cash flow. This means that working capital will be needed. It could come from an overdraft, a bank loan, the business owner's own pocket or retained profit (profits from the past that have been saved to cover future needs).

Calculating cash flow

Figure 12: Calculating cash flow

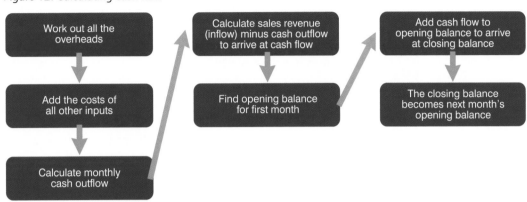

Figure 12 shows how a cash flow chart is created. A typical cash flow forecast for a business starting out is shown below. For illustration purposes the business has both cash sales and credit sales. The assumption is that payment for credit sales will be made two months after the sale. The opening balance and the closing balance will tally with the bank statement. The closing balance is what people mean when they talk about the bottom line: it is the crucial evidence of the month by month security of the business.

Cash flow chart

Cash Flow Forecast for Hire Tools & Gadgets

Receipts £	Jan	Feb	Mar	Apr	May	June	July	Aug	Sep
Cash Sales	200	500	500	500	600	700	700	800	800
Credit Sales	0	0	2400	2700	3000	4000	4000	4500	4700
Capital	5000								
Total	5200	500	2900	3200	3600	4700	4700	5300	5500
Payments									
Suppliers	1040	1280	1400	1800	1840	2080	2160	2200	2320
Salaries	800	800	800	800	800	800	800	800	800
Rent & Rates	400	400	400	400	400	400	400	400	400
Gas/Elec	100	100	100	100	100	100	100	100	100
Advertising	50	50	50	30	30	30	30	30	30
Insurance	100	100	100	100	100	100	100	100	100
Repairs	0	0	0	50	0	0	50	0	50
Telephone	25	25	25	25	25	25	25	25	25
Miscellaneous	20	20	20	20	20	20	20	20	20
Total	2535	2775	2895	3325	3315	3555	3685	3675	3845
Net Cash Flow	2665	-2275	5	-125	285	1145	1015	1625	1655
Opening balance	0	2665	390	395	270	555	1700	2715	4340
Closing balance	2665	390	395	270	555	1700	2715	4340	5995

(questions overleaf)

Questions

1. No receipts for credit sales are shown for January and February. Why is this?

2. Why are the forecasts for salaries, and rent and rates, the same each month?

3. Calculate what the closing balance would have been in each month if the owner had not paid in capital at the start of the business.

4. Are these figures likely to be accurate? Explain your answer.

5. What is the purpose of a cash flow forecast?

6. At no stage of this cash flow forecast does the closing bank balance 'go into the red' therefore overdraft facilities were not needed. Was this wise? Discuss.

7. Complete the cash flow forecast for the remaining 3 months of the year, taking into account the trends shown. There is no 'correct' solution but you must justify your figures.

Using cash flow forecasts

There is often a tendency for businesses to be over-optimistic when forecasting how much cash will come into a business. This may be done with the best intentions but is unlikely to convince a bank manager that the owner has a sound grasp of business essentials. Owners should strive to seek information on which forecasts can be based. If an owner is using cash flow forecasts to convince a bank manager to provide overdraft facilities, it may be advisable to present a range of forecasts. Whereas expenses, if estimated correctly, are unlikely to alter by much, the same cannot be said for sales.

The owners may present the bank with a worst case scenario, a middle range scenario, and a best case scenario. In doing this not only will they show the bank that they have a grasp of the situation, but they will be able to see for themselves what will happen if their plans do not materialise, or do not do so as quickly as expected. Going into business can be demanding mentally and physically and it is best to be well prepared.

The cash flow forecast is a vital addition to the array of information that can be used to help businesses make decisions. Identifying cash shortfalls on a monthly basis can help businesses to seek reasons for the shortfalls and to see if a pattern is emerging. The more information available to the owner, the less likely it is that the same problems will keep occurring. Information creates a better understanding of the situation and the owner can use it to seek ways of improving the situation. **Negative cash flows** can lead to business failure in a very short time unless additional finance can be arranged. In thinking about solutions, you will need to look back at the work you did on Unit 1, Sources of Finance. There is more detail on this in Chapter 14.

> **Negative cash flow** means that cash is flowing out of the business faster than it is coming in. In the chart on page 65, cash flow is negative in February because the business has made credit sales for which no payment has yet come in.

Chapter 13 **Budgets**

Using budgets to plan

Starting a business venture is a daunting task. In the real world it must almost appear insurmountable at times. Most of the high street banks provide information packs (if they agree to provide business accounts and finance facilities in the first place) and there are various business networks and local support groups designed to provide advice. Grants for setting up in a particular area and grants for training may be available, but despite all this the move to setting up a business meets many obstacles. And this is before dealings with Her Majesty's Revenue and Customs (HMRC) have begun.

To minimise risk of failure – a topic that will crop up regularly in this unit – anyone starting a new business needs an appreciation of what their business can do to enhance the chances of success. That, in a nutshell, is what this section of Unit 2A is about. A **budget** is a plan, thought out in advance and set out in numerical terms. It shows target levels of costs and revenues, and provides evidence of the entrepreneur's thinking. A bank may require a budget before providing a loan.

For many small, new businesses it might seem pointless to try to estimate costs and revenues. The owner's time might be far better spent talking with potential customers or suppliers. There is no past experience on which to base estimates. If you think about the fish and chip shop in Chapter 1, you can see why a budget might be best left until later. But for an established business, a budget can highlight the differences between expectations and reality, and provide pointers as to what should happen next.

> A **budget** is a financial plan which forecasts costs and revenues and maps projected changes. It can be used by the management to keep control of the business. An income, or sales, budget sets out expected sales revenue. An expenditure or production budget sets targets for costs, and may include wages.

A sales budget

Selling jewellery

Mary Lewis produced her own hand-made jewellery using African designs. She sold her goods in three categories (bracelets, earrings and necklaces), some on market stalls but more and more via retail outlets. In her second year of business she drew up a sales budget for her designs.

Sales budget	October	November	December
Bracelets	£200	£300	£500
Earrings	£160	£320	£480
Necklaces	£225	£375	£750

Mary was in her second year of business when she prepared these budgets. The months leading up to Christmas were her best months the previous year but the budget was complicated by the fact that she now supplied her goods to retail outlets and she was never sure how much promotion the retailer would give. Margins on jewellery sold in shops were lower as the shopkeeper had to be paid. She anticipated that, in the run up to Christmas, sales would be split 50/50 between her weekend market stall and craft fairs on the one hand, and between retail outlets on the other. Whilst receipts would be immediate on her stalls she anticipated a month's delay before revenue from retailers would arrive.

Questions

1. Mary's sales budget was based on historical information. What does this mean?

2. How might a sales budget help Mary?

Comparing budgets and forecasts

A budget is a plan, while a forecast is a prediction of what might happen in the future. There is a difference. A budget shows what the business aims to achieve. Most budgets are prepared annually and may be adjusted at various points in the light of actual information. They may be set up monthly or even weekly, depending on the size of an organisation. Budgets may be set up for any business variables. Often a budget will cover sales revenue, production costs, profit, personnel, cash and capital expenditure.

A small business like Mary's might first devise some forecasts, probably for sales revenue. From these forecasts, budgets can be set up to help control the business. A budget gives all those in a business a focus, a plan that it aims to achieve, incorporating realistic figures.

For many firms the sales budget will be the first budget to be completed. If a firm has good relations with its existing customers then this budget may be easy to complete. Mary knew what her sales had been in the previous year. Historical information, whilst not foolproof, provides a guide to help prepare accurate budgets.

A firm that is just starting up, or one that relies on the general public for its business, may find estimating sales harder than would a manufacturer with a regular base of clients. A firm selling mainly on credit, invoicing in arrears, will find it advisable to show the expected revenue in the month when it is most likely to be received, rather than the month of the actual sale. This will reflect the delay in payment which can be up to 3 months.

Comparing the budget with reality

Mary's actual sales figures

	October	November	December
Bracelets	£220	£330	£510
Earrings	£200	£400	£600
Necklaces	£285	£480	£875

These results were encouraging. Sales at the retail outlets held up, i.e. they were broadly in line with budgeted figures, but sales at stalls were approximately 50 per cent higher than budget. Mary was good on the craft side and was able to increase her production without too much difficulty. She was mainly worried about her ability to sell – and that seemed not to be a problem.

Questions

1. Mary's sales from her market stalls were higher than the previous year's figures. What might have accounted for this? *(If you can't think of at least 3 reasons, you're not trying!)*
2. Was it a good idea for Mary to seek retail outlets to stock her jewellery?

A budget for the next year should be set up before the end of the current year, otherwise there will be a time gap and the firm will lose some focus. Budgets can be used to make comparisons between the budgeted figures and the actual figures. This will help identify what has gone wrong, and right, and can provide lessons for the future. Possible problem areas for the future may be identified when the firm's performance has failed to keep up with the budgeted performance. In Mary's case, the actual figures compared well with the budget and indicated that her marketing decisions were correct.

Production (or expenditure) budgets

Production budgets may also be called expenditure budgets. They can be used to set a maximum target figure for costs. The sales and production figures together can be used to calculate profit figures and create a profit budget.

Many firms in the tertiary sector will not need a production budget but will buy in goods ready made. For example, a supermarket will add a percentage mark-up to the price they paid, which will determine their selling price. This will reflect the service they give and any expertise they may be able to add on. These firms, however, will still need a purchasing budget, which will set out the costs of the products they will sell.

Production budget	October	November	December
Bracelets	£120	£200	£40
Earrings	£120	£180	£45
Necklaces	£175	£350	£140

Mary made her products a month before she budgeted to sell them. This meant that her production budget for October reflected her anticipated sales for November; that for November reflected budgeted sales for December, whilst production in December reflected budgeted sales for January.

Questions

1. What is the most likely reason for the production budget for December being much lower than that of October and December?

2. Produce a profit budget for November and December.

3. How likely is it that Mary would be pleased with these figures?

4. What kinds of problems might Mary face in the next quarter, January–March?

Achieving targets

Using budgets to manage effectively

Budgets can be very useful in keeping a small business focused on its targets. In a large business they have a particular role in allowing careful monitoring of departmental activity. A production department can be given a budget that sets maximum levels for costs incurred. If the production manager wants to spend more, this will have to be discussed with the senior managers, and carefully justified in terms of possible savings later or quality improvements that would add value to the product.

A marketing department might be given a sales budget that set a minimum level for sales revenue. If this level is not reached then the department would have to explain the reasons and show how the sales might be increased in the future.

Budgets need to be consistent with financial forecasts for profit and cash flow. The figures can be carefully built into budgets for each department of the business. Senior managers can monitor the implications of all its activities and can take action if targets are not being met. If a department has performed well and added to profits by keeping costs below budget or exceeding a revenue target, their good practice can be identified and used to learn lessons for the future.

Variance analysis

Detailed budgets are used to compare actual figures with the budgeted ones. A variance in budgeting is the difference between the budgeted figures and the actual figures. It can give a timely warning that something may be going wrong, while there is time to take action and make changes.

Budgets need to be consistent with financial forecasts for profit and cash flow.

> **Variances** can be favourable or adverse. A favourable variance is one where the actual figures are better than the budgeted ones. An adverse variance is where the actual figures are worse than the budgeted ones.

Mike Elliot specialises in the repair of Alpha Romeo cars

£	March Budget	March Actual	April Budget	April Actual	May Budget	May Actual
Wages	2,000	2,000	2,000	2,000	2,000	2,000
Materials	1,250	1,000	1,250	1,300	1,250	1,450
Advertising	100	100	100	100	100	125
Motor expenses	250	300	250	325	250	350
Other overheads	200	175	200	170	200	180
Total Costs	3,800	3,575	3,800	3,895	3,800	4,105

Questions

1. Calculate the total cost variance for the 3 month period.

2. Is this variance favourable or adverse? Explain your answer.

3. Why do you think the budgeted and actual figures for wages are identical?

4. Identify an example of a favourable variance and an adverse variance from the figures provided.

5. The actual figure for 'materials' is different each month. Outline possible reasons for this.

6. Should Mike Elliot be concerned by what the comparison between budgeted and actual figures reveal?

Using variances

Different businesses use variances in different ways. Large businesses will have very complex budgets because they have many departments. Variances offer managers a way of observing trends and events. How they react depends on the culture of the company. An autocratic leader can use variances to keep very tight control of everything that goes on. A more democratic approach would involve departments in the setting of targets, and foster discussion about how improvements can be made. This would be more in tune with measures to promote continuous improvement.

Setting budgets

An **extrapolation** of figures is simply assuming a trend will continue. For example if sales for a 3 year period were £10,000, £20,000, and £30,000, an extrapolation for the fourth year would be £40,000. (It might be necessary to allow for inflation to make this meaningful.) This example of sales budgeting may be feasible but it could also be lazy as it may not take into account changes, such as growth or recession in the economy. Or it may fail to consider consumer tastes and changes in preferences.

Budgets do need to be considered alongside other evidence about the performance of the business. For example, market research may be used to help decide what might be reasonable targets for sales revenue, or help to explain why a target has not been met. Information about the economy as a whole might give early warning of probable production cost increases arising from inflation or changes in world prices of particular inputs, or simply explain cost increases after the event.

> **Extrapolation** means using data from the recent past and assuming that any trend that can be seen will continue into the future. Provided nothing unexpected happens it will work well in the near future.

Zero based budgeting (ZBB)

Even when the majority of budgeted items are based around historic costs there may be costs that are difficult to quantify. In these cases no money is allocated – the budget is zero based. Each manager in charge of an area must justify each spending item, usually by outlining its benefits. So an accountant in the firm may suggest that computerising the stock control system, whilst likely to be costly and difficult to predict in terms of cost, will be justified in the end due to the value of savings over a period of time.

It is important to emphasise that any past expenditure in a particular area is discounted or ignored when using the zero budgeting approach. Each item of expenditure in an area must be justified before it can be accepted. This makes it a time-consuming way to set the budget, even though it does ensure that costs have been kept as low as possible. Some businesses use zero based budgets for some years but not others – in between they can save time and money by basing the budget on the previous year's experience. ZBB is useful when changes are happening, so that past needs are no longer relevant. It can be used when costs must be cut. But it is time consuming for managers.

> **Zero based budgeting** means starting with no budget and requiring each department to analyse its needs and costs. Budgets can then be structured around current requirements, regardless of what was spent in the past.

Discussion point

What kinds of expenditure might be so difficult to predict that zero-based budgeting is used?

Using budgets

The following case study shows how a budget might be used to address staffing needs. This shows how budgets can be used to keep control of wage and salary costs

The Garden Centre

The budget	Jan		Feb		Mar	
	Number	Cost	Number	Cost	Number	Cost
Full time staff	10	£8,000	10	£8,000	12	£9,600
Part time staff	6	£1,440	6	£1,440	8	£1,920
Total Cost		£9,440	£	9,440		£11,520
Actual figures						
Full time staff	10	£8,800	10	£8,800	12	£12,200
Part time staff	4	£1,200	4	£1,200	4	£1,200
Total Cost		£10,000		£10,000		£13,400

The garden centre employs the same number of full time staff and fewer part-time staff yet the wage bill increases above the budgeted level. The budget may be entirely reasonable yet a failure to attract part-time staff has led to a situation where some full-time members of staff have had to work extra hours at busy times and have been paid a higher rate for doing so. An apparently simple situation like this may be made even more difficult to deal with if the business is just starting out and there is no historical information to call on.

Questions

1. Could the staffing problem have been predicted?

2. What should the management do to avoid this in the future?

Chapter 14 Managing working capital

Cash flow and working capital

Fixing the heating

Pete Wilson is a gasman or more correctly he was a gasman, a self-employed heating engineer. Having been made redundant by one of the large suppliers Pete spent half his redundancy money on a new van and half on a training course to upgrade his skills.

Pete started up as a sole trader and with contacts already established in the area, and with the gift of the gab, he soon found customers. He was good at his job and orders poured in. Pete found himself working a 7-day week, 12 hours a day. He was prepared to do this for a period of time to get his business a good reputation.

With a full order book Pete was feeling good. He got his girlfriend to invoice clients with a 30 day credit period. Unfortunately she did not have the time to do this immediately so sometimes customers were getting up to two months credit.

In the meantime, Pete, because he had no trading track record, had to pay up front for his materials. His cash flow situation became desperate but he managed to secure overdraft facilities on the basis that he had plenty of orders. Money came in slowly, a couple of customers never paid him at all, and he soon reached the upper end of his overdraft limit. He had no cash to pay suppliers, neither could he repay his borrowings and he went bust. Pete's experience is a cautionary tale to all those seeking to open their own business.

Questions

1. Why were Pete's suppliers unwilling to give him credit?

2. What would be the implications for the bank if it had increased Pete's overdraft?

3. Being a sole trader means being the only owner of a business but it doesn't necessarily mean being the only worker in a business. Should Pete have employed someone to run the clerical side of the business? Explain your answer.

Working capital is the money a business needs to pay its short term expenses. These include:

- expenditure like Pete's training
- any raw materials or stocks of inputs
- bills, e.g. for electricity or petrol
- wages, e.g. enough for Pete to live on.

All businesses need working capital. You can see how much working capital a business has by looking at the balance sheet. Working capital is more or less covered by three items, stock (i.e. stocks of inputs or output), debtors (i.e. money owed to the business) and cash in the bank. (There is an example on page 74.)

Working capital is the money needed to keep going in the time gap between paying out cash for all the input costs incurred during production and the time when sales revenue comes in from the customers.

Balance sheet: a statement of the firm's assets and liabilities. Assets add to the value of the business. Liabilities are loans that may have to be repaid.

72

How much working capital is needed?

The amount of working capital held by a business will vary depending on:

- the type of business
- the credit terms a business may be able to negotiate from suppliers
- the credit it extends to customers.

A new business like Pete's may not be able to negotiate any credit period; cash on delivery may be demanded. This may mean that it is not possible to extend credit to customers. However, customers that have some market power (e.g. supermarkets or other businesses) may be able to insist on payment 30 or 60 days after invoicing. It may be necessary to raise working capital to provide this credit.

In general, manufacturing businesses need much more working capital than businesses in the service sector. Dyson has to pay for product development, which is very costly, long before production starts and sales revenue comes in. An antique shop or an advertising agency can rent premises and be selling to customers within a few weeks.

A business with too little working capital may end up with a negative cash flow. But holding too much working capital may be costly and wasteful. Monitoring the use of working capital may save money.

Figure 13: Too little working capital

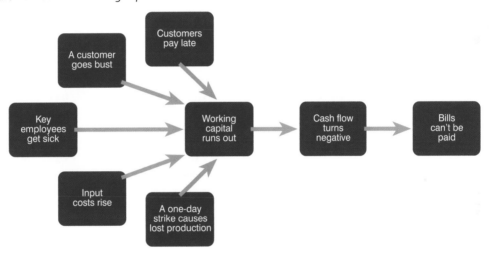

Working capital in the accounts

In accounting terms, working capital can be calculated by deducting **current liabilities** from **current assets**. Current assets consist mainly of stock, debtors (money that will be paid in) and cash held at the bank. Current liabilities are mainly creditors (money that is owed). The concept 'current' refers to a short period of time, usually a year. An asset is something a business owns and a liability is something a business owes.

An accountant might suggest that the ratio of current assets to current liabilities should be 2:1, i.e. that firms should hold twice the value of current assets to current liabilities. Given that a good deal of the value of current assets used to be tied up in stocks, and that generally firms hold fewer stocks now due to the adoption of JIT stock management, the ratio is usually much lower. Firms should still aim to have sufficient working capital to pay for their short term debts.

> **Current liabilities** are short-term loans that must be paid within a year or less. They include overdrafts and any trade credit offered by suppliers.
>
> **Current assets** include stocks of inputs or output, debts to the company that will bring in cash in the future, and cash at the bank.

Garden centres

Compare the following components of working capital for two garden centres.

Garden Needs		Sunshine Gardens	
Stock	£20000	Stock	£10000
Debtors	10000	Debtors	4000
Bank	10000	Bank	4000
	40000		18000
Current Liabilities		Current Liabilities	
Creditors	10000	Creditors	6000
	£30000		£12000

Question

Which of the two garden centres has the best working capital position?

Before answering the question consider the following points:

Both businesses have positive working capital, i.e. they are able to pay off their short term debts quite easily.

It could be argued that Garden Needs is in a better position, and it may be. It appears to have a good level of stock, plenty of money owing to it and a healthy bank balance. But why is it carrying so much stock? How long has it had the stock for? Will the stock deteriorate? Why has it got so much owing to it? Does it chase up debts well? Why have all that money lying in the bank? Can it not be made to work? And why, considering the points made already, does it still owe £10,000?

Garden Needs' current ratio (the ratio of current assets to current liabilities) is 4:1, compared to Sunshine Gardens ratio of 3:1. Both these ratios would be considered good but perhaps too high. Sunshine Gardens holds lower stock levels, is owed less money and carries less 'spare' money in the bank. Its creditors, whilst lower than Garden Needs, are higher than the amount in the bank and if the creditors demanded quick payment it would not be able to comply without realising some of its other current assets. Consider your verdict.

Recession

How problems develop

Businesses that use detailed budgets will examine variances carefully and will get an idea of how well they are doing. What that doesn't show is how quickly cash is coming into a business and how quickly it is going out. Only when actual cash flows are compared with forecasted cash flows will it become clear if a firm is cash rich or cash poor. Firms with a good system of variance analysis and cash flow management will be able to react quickly to cash flow shortages.

When the economy is doing well businesses do not necessarily need to be as cash rich as they do when the economy is not doing well. Some businesses perform well in hard times; discount stores and supermarkets that concentrate on non-branded products are two examples. But most businesses find that they have fewer customers and they are spending less. Having cash available in times of hardship is a godsend for businesses. In 2008, many businesses fortunately had savings from the good years. If they had not, the recession would have been much worse.

When the market is growing, many businesses will want to expand to take advantage of the demand for their products. But long before they can sell the final product, they have to have funds to cover their costs of production. If they expand faster than they can pay their bills, they are said to be **overtrading**. This was probably what happened to Pete in the opening case study. Business owners need to know, either from past experience or from the signals in their monthly cash flow, when they will need to inject extra finance into their business.

Overtrading

> **Overtrading** occurs when a business, especially a new business, rapidly expands, taking in orders that cannot be supported by its working capital. This can have serious repercussions.

Contingency finance planning

Contingency finance planning should be in place before any crises are identified. There are several possibilities and the first port of call may not be the bank. Other measures include:

- managing supplier credit
- managing customer credit
- can stocks be reduced?
- factoring.

Banks are out to make profits for their shareholders and much of that profit comes from business customers. Rather than rushing to the bank, businesses should make sure they have reviewed their internal procedures first.

Customer relationships

Good relationships with customers and suppliers are vital. If a business always pays suppliers on time, doesn't always wait 30 days or more before paying, it can expect those suppliers to reciprocate when times are hard. After all, suppliers need customer businesses to stay afloat. Negotiating extended credit terms would be worthwhile but businesses that have not been good payers cannot expect favours. Supplies may be cut off.

Can customers be persuaded to pay up more quickly? Even if only a few comply with this request, a cash crisis may be averted. Giving better discounts to those who do pay quickly can give them an incentive to pay quickly.

If stocks can be reduced, less working capital will be needed. The flow chart shows how JIT stock control might allow destocking, save money and free up working capital for other things.

There is no one magic figure for the right level of working capital. Having more might make it possible to run the business more efficiently or buy inputs in bulk, so that prices can be cut and sales increase. Or it might be possible to buy from a cheaper supplier that does not offer credit terms. Being able to offer extended credit to customers might help to keep customers who would otherwise go elsewhere.

Managing working capital is vital to the business. But having more is not necessarily the answer to a cash flow problem. It might be better to use existing working capital more effectively – by any method mentioned above.

Factoring

If a business has had some difficulty collecting debts, or cannot find the time to chase them up, **factoring** may provide an answer. Factors specialise in taking over debts from businesses in this position. The business 'sells' the debt to the factor, who will collect it later. The business gets a payment that is less than the amount of the bill. If the debtor is generally a regular payer, the factor may pay an amount close to the value of the debt. If the debt is more toxic, the amount received will be lower.

Factoring means passing the debt to someone else in return for a proportion of its value. The factor (which may be a department of the bank) will assume responsibility for collecting the debt. It will pay the business the amount of the debt, less a discount that reflects the risk they are taking on and the length of time before payment.

Borrowing

An overdraft or a loan?

Many businesses seek **overdraft** facilities from their bank to help tide them over in the initial months of slow growth. Other businesses, especially if they face seasonal sales fluctuation, may need overdraft facilities when trade is slow. A condition of receiving overdraft facilities, i.e. the ability to make payments over and above the amounts available in the business bank account, often states that the business owner must inject some capital of their own into the business bank account.

An overdraft is an agreement between bank and client that allows the clients to make payments up to an agreed limit, over and above what is in that account. Banks will give new customers free banking for a period of time, usually a year, but then they will start to make money. Usually there is the monthly service charge. As soon as the business draws on its overdraft facility, interest charges will be incurred. It is true that they are only raised for the period of time that the account is overdrawn but in times of recession that may be a long time for many firms.

Overdraft: a loan facility offered by banks whereby businesses (and individuals) can make payments, up to a certain limit, even when there is no cash in the account.

The rate of interest on an overdraft is usually higher than that on a loan and woe betide any business that exceeds its overdraft limit. Further interest will be charged and that may include interest on the interest, as well as a charge for exceeding the limit. If cheques bounce there will be more charges.

This is a very gloomy scenario, a kind of self-fulfilling prophecy. Overdrafts that are managed well are very useful for businesses, getting them out of short-term cash flow problems, but they certainly should not be used to cure long-term structural problems, such as replacing unprofitable facilities.

Loans

Loans involve borrowing a fixed sum of money, repayable in fixed amounts, each repayment bearing a proportion of the interest charge, over a fixed period of time, two years or five years for instance. In this they are similar to mortgages. They provide a degree of certainty for the borrower, as they know when and how much they will be paying out each month. The interest rate is generally lower than that on an overdraft although interest is paid on the full amount for the period of the loan, even though the full amount is not owed for that full period. If the loan brings rewards in terms of extra income and profit, it can be paid off early, thus removing some of the interest burden.

Business loans are generally provided for specific purposes such as the purchase of a machine, or vehicle, or other fixed asset. They help manage working capital in that they should bring long term rewards to a business, thus enhancing the chances of positive cash flow. A new machine may lead to faster production processes at a lower cost per unit, so saving the firm money and bringing in extra revenue. Loans may help with contingency finance planning if they lead fairly quickly to an improved cash flow position. An investment that successfully delivers extra sales revenue and profit will increase working capital.

Monitoring stocks

Show what you know

1. Explain, in your own words, the difference between a loan and an overdraft.
2. Draw up a table showing the advantages and disadvantages of loans and overdrafts.
3. Some events cannot be predicted with any certainty. Therefore contingency finance planning may be needed. In what circumstances might an overdraft or a delay in paying a supplier be seen as an example of contingency finance planning?
4. Why is it important for firms to monitor their working capital?
5. What dangers might face firms that rely too heavily on loans and overdrafts to keep their businesses afloat?

Holding appropriate levels of stock

Holding excessive stocks has an **opportunity cost**. People in business have to make big decisions all the time. How much to invest? Whether to expand? Whether to continue? Choosing the right level of stock to hold may not seem such a big issue but for many businesses, and not just those selling perishables, it is.

> **Opportunity cost** is the next best or highest value alternative that has to be foregone. The opportunity cost of reading this text might be studying another subject, or playing on a games console, or watching Liverpool beat Manchester United, or just chilling.

Regardless of the length of time someone has been in business, decisions about how much stock to hold are a major concern. If a business sells from its existing stock of goods, it will have to hold enough stock to avoid feeling nervous. This applies to all sizes of business regardless of whether they are storing stock in a garage or in a highly computerised warehouse. Many businesses now use JIT stock systems but they can go wrong and they put pressure on the supplier to have goods ready 'now'. As we have seen, that can lead to quality levels falling.

Have you ever been to a car boot sale and run out of items immediately? Did you misjudge demand? Did you sell at the wrong price? Or have you been stuck there for hours and not shifted a thing until you reduced your prices? Did you have the right 'stock'? If you are comfortable with your stock level you may have too much. If you are feeling nervous all the time, you probably have too little.

Even firms who know their business inside out can get stock levels wrong. If a firm loses a sale because they have run out of stock that is not just annoying, it is a waste of advertising, labour and, of course, sales revenue. If a firm has unsold stock for too long, it risks never being able to sell it, perhaps due to technology or fashion changes. It has also spent money that could have been used elsewhere. This is why stock levels must be monitored regularly.

Boden

The British fashion outlet Boden opened in 1991, employs 800 people and ships 12,500 parcels out of its warehouse in Leicester every day. It has this advice for customers, particularly those who have not been able to buy an item because it is not in stock. "The most common cause of bankruptcy among retail outlets is holding too much stock. Even if we wanted to, we couldn't order much more stock than we do currently as we couldn't afford it. It would mean much more 'Sale' activity – good for you, but ultimately suicidal for us."

Questions

1. Illustrate, using you own examples, the concept of opportunity cost.
2. If stock levels are such a big problem, why don't all firms hold buffer stocks?
3. Why, according to Boden, is 'holding too much stock' the most common cause of bankruptcy among retail outlets?
4. Which is the best stock control system – JIT, buying to order, or holding a buffer stock? (I would hope to see the words 'it depends' somewhere in your answer.)

Chapter 15

The difference between cash and profit

A hotel in Wales

Owen and Jenna Thomas both lost their jobs and received redundancy payments at the same time. They decided to put the money into starting a hotel business in a beautiful spot in North Wales. They got a loan and overdraft facilities from the bank. They started taking guests in the spring of 2005 and in the first three years they did well. Cash flow and profit were both strong and they were as well off as they had been when working for their old employers.

The summer of 2008 was a good one. Then in the autumn the financial crisis developed and winter bookings dropped away. Cash flow was negative but the couple did not worry because they already knew that they had made a good profit for the year. Even if sales revenue was down a bit in 2009, they would still be profitable.

Early in the new year, they began to receive bookings for the summer. Clearly some people were going to holiday in Wales rather than more exotic places. They could see ways of surviving the coming recession with special offers. But the bank did not wait. It could see from the bank statements that cash flow was negative and it pulled the plug. It withdrew the overdraft facility and refused to consider whether profits might return in the summer.

Questions

1. Why did the owners think the business could survive through 2009?

2. What would make the bank choose to withdraw the overdraft when the business still looked profitable?

Negative cash flow and losses

Profit and cash

- Profit is the difference between total sales revenue and total costs. If that figure is negative a loss has been made.

- Cash flow is the difference between the inflow of cash and the outflow, usually in the space of a month. Cash flow may also be negative, but then it may be positive the next month. Usually, cash flow would be negative over a longer period of time if losses are being made.

Sales revenue is the money received from customers. Cash inflow is different – it may include a bank loan, or cash invested by the business owner, or the proceeds from the sale of an asset, e.g. a van or an office building. Similarly, the cash outflow may include dividend payments or a loan repayment, not just business expenses. A profit and loss account measures profit and cash flow measures cash inflows and outflows. They are linked, but different.

Unfortunately for the hotel in Wales, the bank was not prepared to wait to see if a profit could be made in the summer. It took the short-run indications from the cash flow figures to mean that there was no hope of profit even in the long run. It was not prepared to run the risks experienced by hotels in a recession.

Both cash flow and profitability are threatened in a recession. Unpaid debts are more likely then. But unpaid debts are a fact of business life – the business that hasn't had any is very lucky indeed.

Some businesses are much more vulnerable than others to cash flow problems, even if they are likely to be profitable in the long run:

- New businesses are likely to find that sales are slow to get started, especially if they take time to get their marketing strategies right.

● Makers of new, technically innovative manufactured products have to invest a lot of cash up front, spending on R&D and production facilities. They need substantial funds.

● Small businesses, e.g. farmers that rely on a few big powerful customers like supermarkets, may face cash flow problems if they lose just one customer.

Cash is the lifeblood of a business – you've heard this before. Businesses can go without profit for a while; some seem to be able to go without profit for a long time, as at Ocado. This works for as long as investors are prepared to back the business, but without cash a business will not survive indefinitely. Money in the bank is needed to pay wages, expenses and materials. Not paying wages would mean disaster; as soon as materials are not paid for suppliers will stop supplying.

Investing

If profit is invested back into a business wisely, especially if it is used in the purchase of fixed assets, then that investment should bear fruit in the future. Purchases of vehicles, of machinery, and of computer controlled systems for stock control or advanced robotic technology, should all create profit in the future, as costs are driven down and profit margins are increased. The purchase of fixed assets is not treated as a business expense in the profit and loss account, so whilst cash balances will be reduced no immediate effect on profits will be recorded.

Timing of payments

You can see that the difference between cash and profit can be traced to the timing of payments. Business accounting is based on the principle that as a sale is made, it is recorded in the accounts. A sale made in the last month of a financial year, say, December, should be recorded in that financial year, but the money for payment may not be received until February, which is in the next financial year. The assumption is that the payment will be made and contribute to profits earned in December.

Trade credit

The timing of payments complicates the relationship between cash and profit. Materials bought using trade credit will appear in the accounts at the time of the transaction but may not be paid for until a later period. The case study below shows how this might affect cash flow and profit.

Selling shoes

Sole to Sole, a shoe retailer, sells in shops by card and cash (both regarded as instant receipts) and to bowling alleys, who take one month to pay. All expenses, including purchases of stock are paid for straight away. The cash flow statement for a quarterly period reveals the following:

	January	February	March
Cash Sales	£5,000	£6,000	£7,000
Credit sales receipts	£7,000	£5,000	£6,000
Total	£12,000	£11,000	£13,000
Expenses			
Purchases	4,000	3,500	4,500
Wages	2,000	2,000	2,000
Other expenses	1,000	1,000	1,000
	7,000	6,500	7,500
Total Cash Flow	5,000	4,500	(a)

(questions overleaf)

Questions

1. Calculate the cash flow figure at (a) for March

2. Calculate the total cash flow for the 3 month period. Show your workings.

3. The credit sales for March were £8,000. Calculate the profit for the 3 month period. Show your workings.

4. Why is there a difference between the profit figure and the net cash flow?

5. If the owner had injected another £5,000 into the business in January how much would the difference be between net cash flow and profit? Show your workings.

If a business has been trading successfully for some time, some of the profit made, perhaps most of it, can be ploughed back into the business. This money will often be used to cover day-to-day expenditure, i.e. as working capital. This may seem disappointing but could bring additional profit in the future.

The owner or owners of a business may be prepared to inject more capital into the business themselves. This is not treated as trading revenue in the profit and loss account and will not be shown to increase profits, even though that injection may lead to future profits. It is however recorded as cash injected into the business – another reason why cash and profit are not the same thing.

Survival

How the numbers work

Cash Registers, a firm selling cash tills to businesses has sales of £650,000 during the year. The cost of purchases and other business expenses amount to £450,000, leaving a profit of £200,000. Sales of £40,000 were made in the last month of the financial year and only £10,000 of that money has been received. Similarly purchases in the last month amounted to £15,000 of which only £5,000 had been paid.

Receipts for the year (ignoring a possible similar situation at the beginning of the year) amount to £650,000 less £40,000, plus £10,000, leaving total cash received of £620,000. Expenditure is £450,000 less £15,000, plus £5,000, leaving a total of £440,000. The profit recorded was £200,000 but the total cash received was £180,000, a difference between profit and cash of £20,000.

Show what you know

A business, in its first year of trading makes sales of £80,000, has total expenses of £50,000. All of its sales were on credit and by the end of the year £20,000 of those sales had not been paid for. Similarly credit purchases of £20,000 had been made and £5,000 of those had not been paid for. Calculate (a) the profit for the business; (b) the amount of cash received, and (c) the difference between the profit and cash received. Show your workings.

The fact is that net cash receipts and profit are hardly ever a problem for firms that are trading profitably. When profit margins are very small then a delay in receiving cash from sales starts to cause problems, as the money is not always there to pay suppliers and staff. When bad debts occur and some customers don't pay at all, and when others pay very slowly, a situation arises that will set alarm bells ringing. It is at this point that overdrafts are used frequently, credit agreements are re-examined, and loans and the factoring of debts may be considered.

No firm can trade indefinitely if making a loss. At some point the owner or creditors, or indeed other investors, will say 'enough is enough'. If the problems are cyclical and the firm is cash rich it may be able to continue trading in the expectation that trade will pick up and all will be well. It is important to realise that ultimately a firm must make profits in order for it to continue to invest, to continue with its trading cycle and in order to make the effort worthwhile. This is why, whilst cash is king in the short term, in the long run, profit matters most.

Selling sportswear

Two old friends set themselves up in business in the 1970s selling sports wear. The leisure side of this industry was only just beginning to catch on then and their sales were mainly to sports teams. In an effort to broaden their appeal, one of the partners, without consulting the other, bought 5,000 pairs of sports socks from a dealer who was cold calling. This was a bad decision on three grounds;

- trust was destroyed between the partners. In law a decision made by one partner is binding on all partners

- the firm was known for selling football kits, not leisure wear

- the socks only fitted small children. Caveat emptor! Which means, let the buyer beware.

The firm closed down soon after. The sports sock decision lost the firm a large amount of money and also damaged the relationship between the two owners.

Questions

1. Consider the reasons why the decision was mistaken. Which was the most important and why?

2. How could this mistake have been avoided?

According to a report from the BBC in October 2010, four out of every five business start-ups ends in failure and often the main cause is either poor planning or a total lack of it. Some businesses that fail, whether they are start-ups or established companies, are unlucky. But usually there are reasons for their failure – and often, the cause is a combination of problems. Most failures fall into at least one of three problem areas:

- Inability to compete

- Being in the wrong location

- Facing changes in market conditions and being unable to adapt.

This chapter takes each category in turn but you will notice that although one failing may stand out from the rest, often there are other less significant problems that have played a part.

Problems with the competition

It is probably not a good idea to go into business just because you have a little bit of knowledge about the goods or services you are providing. Planning should be detailed and owners must ask themselves if they have the business experience to deal with all aspects of the business. If not, and they don't have a family member to help, then they need to hire someone who does have the necessary experience and that doesn't come cheap.

Problems can come from weak management skills or lack of experience in any aspect of the business. Ineffective market research, poor inventory (stock) management or weaknesses in training could all make the business less efficient and raise costs of production. This in turn will affect profitability. It is not just small and medium sized firms that can be hit by poor management. Very big businesses often face problems and ultimately if they cannot generate cash they will go under.

- Thorough **market research**, conducted before starting up, a business could get an early warning of intense competition in the market place. Entrepreneurs must take steps to ensure that they do actually have a market in which their product will sell. They may otherwise overestimate expected sales, perhaps due to poor planning. This may be caused by naivety and over-confidence. Studying the market could lead to better planning, sensible production targets and appropriate advertising strategies. This type of approach would have helped the business in the case study above. If you think about Jack and the fish and chip shop on page 3 it is clear that the previous owners of the shop did not do their market research.

Reputation

- **Poor inventory management** – the inability of a firm to manage its stocks properly – is a common reason for failure. Business to business (B2B) deals are less likely to be renewed if one firm lets down another. This is because the profits and reputation of the customer firm are directly affected when the supplier fails to deliver. The firm losing out will quickly drop an inefficient supplier, or one that doesn't have the right type of goods, in favour of a firm that can supply quality and quantity as and when required. Reputation is often difficult to establish and no business wants to lose it through the fault of another firm. Individual consumers may be prepared to wait for delivery but in a fast moving world that is becoming less likely as well. Poor inventory management figured in the story of the business supplying board games on page 47. JIT doesn't work unless it is well managed.

- A similar problem – **oversupply** – can also cause problems. Firms buying in large quantities of inputs, often with the best intentions, e.g. because they were offered discount for bulk buying, can find themselves with deteriorating cash flow.

Weak management

- Weak management of **cash flow** may cause a new business to fail very quickly. Remember Pete the plumber on page 72? Because he did not ensure that he got paid as quickly as possible, he ran out of cash to pay for his plumbing supplies.

- As a business grows it may need to **recruit staff**. This can be difficult and costly but employing the wrong person can be disastrous. Do you have a part-time job? Are you a good employee? Do you turn up on time? Do you meet the general public in your job? Do you have a friendly disposition? First impressions count. Not every business customer or potential customer will be easy to deal with. The first meeting with a potential customer can make or break the deal. Courteous staff are very important to the firm.

Some of the fastest growing firms make enormous efforts to train and treat their staff well because they know that their staff are as important as their customers. Unfortunately some firms don't make the effort and this is reflected in poor customer service and inevitably, a deteriorating reputation.

Weak management of cash flow may cause a new business to fail very quickly.

1. Why is efficient stock management important to a business?

2. Business owners with a poor attitude to staff and customers will produce a poor product or service. Discuss.

3. Can a business owner who is responsible for every aspect of the business be efficient?

Location

Selling snakes

I was recently asked to advise on the setting up of a business dealing in aquatics and reptiles – exotic species of fish and slimy creatures. The plan was to set up in a busy retail shopping area. I asked the owner how many of his sales would be from passing trade and he replied, 'very few'. Clearly there was no need to be in this area. Not only was the rent relatively high but also there was very little space for parking.

I was surprised to see the level of demand for this type of business. In such a specialised area, customers are usually willing to travel to less commercially busy spots, with better access, to browse the merchandise. Incidentally, I advised that as in all businesses, relevant insurance is a necessity, but in this trade when live creatures are transported from round the world and many don't survive the journey, specialist insurance is essential, and its cost had better be absorbed into the selling price of every 'product'.

Question

What other types of business could flourish outside the main shopping areas? Give three examples and explain.

Competition

One reason often given for the closure of a business is being in the wrong location. Placing an antiques shop next to a row of '£ shops' selling low value goods is probably not a good choice. But many independent stores are being squeezed from the high street due to a combination of high rents and cut throat prices from large national competitors. Even independent convenience stores that are well away from the high street are being threatened by mini-supermarkets, e.g. Tesco Metro. There are often protests about this, but the popularity of local Sainsbury and Tesco seems to suggest that the decline is irreversible. Some market towns, perhaps conscious of their appeal to tourists, both local and international, have resisted the call for uniformity but this may not be for long.

Some businesses do make mistakes over location. They set up without doing their research, without even doing footfall counts, or without sufficient advertising of their location. They make choices that defy logic. In busy areas the turnover may not cover the rent for the premises. If it will not cover the other fixed costs, the business is doomed.

Find out more

Look back at pricing strategies in Chapter 4 and the work you did on contribution costing in Unit 1. Work out what measures might be useful for a business that is not covering its costs in a high street location.

Diminishing demand

Location problems

The results of research carried out by CB Richard Ellis, a property consultant, released in September 2011, suggest that Britain's high streets are becoming increasingly barren as more and more stores close. The report suggested that the decline of the high street was down to a number of factors, including retail business failures (caused by a number of factors) and changing shopping patterns.

Jonathan De Mello, CBRE's head of retail consultancy stated that "the age of giant shopping centres and major regional shopping malls is having a significant impact on small towns and secondary shopping centres." It may not be possible to reverse this trend. The survey found that only four of the UK's top 74 largest cities and towns were able to stem the tide of high street closures. The worse affected town centre was Margate with 37.4 per cent of shops empty. In Rotherham there was a rise in boarded up units of 13.7 per cent in only six months.

The growing North-South divide was evident with 90 per cent of the 25 largest towns with the highest vacancy rates in the Midlands and North. The only positive news was in Manchester where the vacancy rate of 19 per cent is not considered excessive for a large city and is holding up well.

Questions

1. For three different types of retail outlet, explain why fewer businesses want to locate in high streets.

2. Given the increasing value of sales coming from on-line selling, to what extent is the location of business premises as important as it used to be? Or is it even more important?

Town and city councils rely on income from business rates. Local business people rely on income to keep them in the area; at the same time their own spending helps to contribute to the wealth of the area. Some of the empty units could be converted into residential space but if an area is to be regenerated it has to be attractive enough for this to be worthwhile. When the economy recovers from the recession, it may be clear that traditional shopping centres can thrive – or not.

Market conditions

Changing market conditions

Night life

The number of bar, pub and nightclub businesses going bust rose by almost a tenth during the second quarter of 2011, compared with the first quarter. Despite a boost from the Royal Wedding, consumer confidence remained weak, curbing consumer spending on entertainment. Disposable incomes have fallen in real terms and uncertainty over job security means people are keeping their purse strings tight, according to Anthony Cork, a partner at the accountancy firm Wilkins Kennedy. He also added that the rise in alcohol duty announced in the Budget had eaten into profit margins.

Many pub landlords are tied to tenancy agreements that determine the prices they can charge. Add to this the availability of relatively cheap alcohol in supermarkets, the ban on smoking in bars and pubs, and perhaps it is not surprising that trade is falling and insolvencies rising.

Question

Have the pub, entertainment and leisure industries been unlucky to see so many closures, or are they the architects of their own downfall?

Supermarkets' ability to buy in bulk and cut prices has affected the profitability of pubs and other outlets for alcohol. These changes in **market conditions** affect all firms, particularly those in the retail sector, and particularly, the independent sector.

> **Market conditions** refer to the characteristics of a market such as the number of competitors, the level of competition, the market's growth rate, the pace of innovation and the level of demand for the product.

Market change and competition

Large shopping malls have little room for small independent businesses which cannot compete on price and cannot pay the high rents. Even some of the larger companies fail to survive: either their range of products or their quality fails to bring in enough customers to justify the prominent location. TJ Hughes is a recent example of this. This does not mean that there isn't a place for large businesses at the cheaper end of the market. Despite criticism regarding the sourcing of their products, Primark has established a strong presence in the market.

Some businesses have the wrong product for the times and there will always be winners and losers in any market place.

- Changes in customer preferences can reduce sales dramatically.
- Some businesses will be unable to compete when more efficient and better managed businesses enter the market and sell for less.
- New technologies change markets too – making some products obsolete.
- Lack of customer demand in a recession, caused by falling or stagnating incomes, is a very significant cause of failure.

Many of the reasons for difficulty in competing have links with aspects of market change. A dynamic business can on its own change the market – think of Dyson and its impact on Hoover and the other manufacturers of vacuum cleaners. But one aspect of market change affects most businesses: recession and reduced spending power have a massive impact. The data from ONS on business closures shows this. For every business that actually fails there will be many others that report reduced profits.

Some businesses – Domino's Pizza is one – actually flourish during a recession. Their pizzas are attractive to customers who would in better times have eaten out or bought more expensive takeaways. This may account for some of Primark's success: profits may fall in a recovery. But far more businesses are likely to experience difficult trading conditions.

In Chapter 7 on pages 39-41 there is a brief overview of the state of the British economy since 2008, and the effect of that on sectors of industry. Businesses faced massive market change.

The impact of recession

Data on business closures is a key indicator of the state of the economy. The table compares sector performance in 2007, when the recession had not yet affected many businesses, and 2011, when most were facing difficulties.

Bankruptcies (by Quarter) forced by trading debts	3rd Quarter 2007	1st Quarter 2011
Construction	380	600 (this peaked at 700 per quarter in 2009)
Transport, storage and Communication	230	270
Wholesale & retail	300	425 (this rose rapidly during 2011)
Restaurants and hotels	160	375
Real estate	80	165

Source: ONS

Questions

1. Rank the sectors according to the extent of the change between 2007 and 2011.

2. Examine the results for the two least and the two worst affected sectors. For each sector, explain how they were affected by the recession and give reasons for the impact in each case.

Recession

When the economy slows down consumers spend less. People who become unemployed will have much lower incomes. Those in work are less likely to get a good pay rise. They may also aim to save more because of fears of further job losses. So some sectors of the economy are badly hit. Many restaurants will struggle no matter how well run they are.

Similarly, when banks stop lending and place more conditions on borrowers, estate agents and the building industry are going to be badly affected. Demand goes down and supply has to adjust accordingly. Less efficient firms may be the first to fail but others will go too. Transport, storage and communication has been surprisingly resilient given the added problems of rising oil prices. Telecommunications, where there is still huge technological change and interest, has held up.

The wholesale and retail sector has performed relatively well until the last two quarters of the survey, but it is in this sector that the most concern about debt levels was expressed. Perhaps profit margins have been squeezed as far as they can be. The Insolvency Service, which takes charge of failing businesses, believes that the bulk of bankruptcies will be individually owned, small businesses not covered by limited liability, who have less flexibility in doing deals with banks, making them an easier target for creditors, including HMRC (the tax authorities).

Show what you know

1. From the evidence presented and from your own research and observations explain the difficulties faced by firms when the level of economic activity slows down.

2. Independent retailers have been hit hard by the intensity of competition. Is there anything they can do to survive or are they all likely to disappear?

3. What types of business are most likely to remain resilient, even in a recession?

Failure

Should I go or should I stay?

HMV has moved in technology, fashion, live music, and cinemas and has the backing of Sony Music, the Ministry of Sound group and EMI Music. At the time of writing it remains profitable and generates net positive cash flows and is a powerful brand. It is the leading seller of CDs and DVDs in the UK. It is almost 'the last man standing' in its market.

In January 2011 it issued a profit warning and announced a plan to sell 60 stores, in an effort to fight back against internet and supermarket competition. Sales at the HMV chain fell 13 per cent in the 10 weeks to January 1st 2011: the weather drove even more shoppers online. Yet the run up to Christmas is usually the chain's busiest period. It even opened 'pop up' stores in busy locations for that period only.

Waterstones, the book seller, is part of the HMV group and sales there held up relatively well but rumours suggest that HMV may have to sell Waterstones as well.

Questions

1. Is HMV a victim of changing market conditions or has it overestimated its potential for sales?

2. Is the decision to sell off 60 of its stores a reflection of poor management of its cash flow position?

3. Is the introduction of off-shoots to its core business likely to breathe new life into the iconic brand? Or should it plan to shrink as sales of CDs will keep on declining?

Centralise or decentralise?

Organisation in the public sector

The NHS was established in the UK in 1948 to provide a comprehensive health service to improve physical and mental health through prevention, diagnosis and treatment. It was always said that this treatment should be 'from cradle to grave'.

Over the years the organisational structure has changed repeatedly as different political parties have tried to get the best value for money from an organisation that now employs over a million people. The existing structure, which is shown in Figure 14 is set for radical alteration by 2012/13. All countries hope to deliver comprehensive, good quality, accessible healthcare at a cost that society is prepared to pay. Internationally, a good health service can be organised in many different ways, for example using insurance, central taxation, local authority management and the private sector.

Figure 14

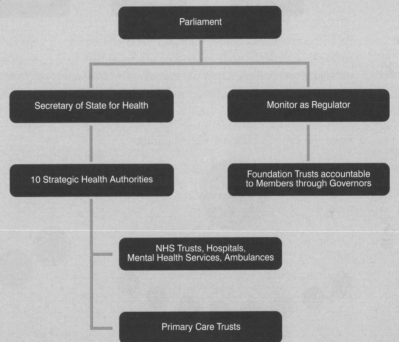

The management of the NHS has alternated between a **centralised** structure and a **decentralised** structure. It is hard to imagine a fully decentralised NHS because ultimately it is accountable to Parliament; also there are huge cost savings to be made from centralised buying. However it is sometimes said that a centralised organisational structure may overlook some of the needs of individual patients.

The latest proposals for change in the NHS organisational structure entail increased power for General Practitioners. This devolvement of power suggests a more decentralised approach. A decentralised structure may mean increasing the number of administrative posts. Patient needs may become a higher priority but at an added cost. Moving back to a centralised structure could leave posts unfilled.

Questions

1. How might patient needs be better served in a decentralised NHS?
2. Could the new system benefit some people more than others? Give examples.

Organisational structures

In all but the smallest of businesses, an **organisational chart** shows the way in which the chain of command works within an organisation. As a business gets larger and functions become more complex the structure will not be so simple. Figure 14 showed an organisation chart for the NHS. Many medium sized businesses would have an organisational structure rather like that shown in Figure 15.

Figure 15: An organisation chart

Centralised decisions

Fast food chains like Burger King and Pizza Hut operate a centralised system which helps them give customers exactly the same experience whenever they visit a particular restaurant. Not only will all stores within a group look alike; they will also have the same quality of food as meals are prepared identically in all outlets. These standardised procedures create cost savings so that unit costs are reduced. Senior managements enjoy greater control over the organisation and there is little room for originality.

Figure 16: Centralisation and decentralisation

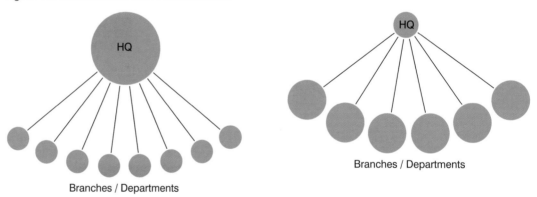

These decisions are made to benefit the organisation as a whole. The fast food industry **franchises** many of its outlets so that all the basic organisational details are dealt with locally. At the same time, the managers have to follow very tight procedures which are all centrally controlled and this guarantees the quality and consistency of the brand. An organisation chart for Pizza Hut would show just a few managers at the top, undertaking centralised tasks, and the many franchises operating independently, carrying out delegated decisions locally.

Centralised decision-taking implies that all decisions are taken at the head office.

Decentralised decisions are taken at the point where the decision will be put into effect.

Organisation charts show how lines of authority work and who is accountable to whom.

Franchises are independent businesses that have the right to sell a branded product.

Supermarkets often attract managers who want to be able to challenge themselves by being involved in the decision making process. This is despite the fact that they do not pay top salaries, compared to other similar sized organisations. They can do this because, for example, Morrisons and Tesco allow managers a degree of autonomy. They are allowed to decide on staffing issues and store promotion, which gives them invaluable experience. This type of experience may be hugely motivational. Also, it allows senior managers to concentrate on group strategy rather than the nitty-gritty of local store management.

Empowerment

The empowerment that is felt by these managers may be transferred lower down the chain as supervisors become involved in the decision making process. Staff are able to use their local knowledge to help stores thrive and can become effective decision makers. Senior managers, based centrally, may not be able react quickly to local circumstances.

Balancing the advantages of decentralisation against centralisation is quite difficult. The choice will depend on the type of firm involved. Many public limited companies (plc's) will rely heavily on experienced senior managers at board level. When the company or the economy as a whole is not doing well, strong leadership will be needed and may be seen as reassuring for staff at lower levels.

Show what you know

1. Why is a more decentralised approach to organisational structure likely to be more costly for a firm or organisation than a centralised system?

2. Is a firm operating an organisational structure that is centralised more likely or less likely to be able to respond quickly to changes in the local environment? Explain your answer.

3. Is Roman Abramovich, the Russian oligarch and owner of Chelsea football club, likely to favour centralisation of the football club or decentralisation? Explain your answer.

4. Consider whether you would prefer to work for a firm that is centrally organised or one that is de-centralised, in each of the following situations:
   - As a 16 year old in your first job
   - As an eighteen year old after 'A' levels or an equivalent qualification
   - As a 21/22 year old with a degree.

The chain of command

You may be familiar with Chinese whispers. An order or instruction is passed along a line, usually by whispering to the person next to you, to see if the end instruction is still the same as it was at the beginning. Often it is not. An old story from the trenches in World War I tells of sending the message, 'send reinforcements we're going to advance', but it gets passed on through so many people that it comes out as 'send three and four pence we're going to a dance'.

A **chain of command** shows the way authority and the power to take decisions are passed down within a business. The most senior people are at the top of it, with layers of more junior people beneath them. Figure 17 shows how a manager might pass on decisions to one or two deputies, who would in turn provide appropriate instructions for individual departments.

If the chain of command is too long, communications get misinterpreted. However if the chain of command is too short the people receiving the message may not fully understand the complexity of the message.

Figure 17 illustrates a short chain of command and a wide **span of control**. A wide span of control offers more responsibility to those at the bottom of the chain and thus could be said to be motivational as it offers **empowerment**. This is not necessarily the same as authority: most of that will be reserved for those higher up the chain. A short chain, by reducing the number of middle managers, may cost less. The hierarchy is flatter, with fewer layers and more opportunities for junior managers to take some decisions. A disadvantage is that it confers responsibility on those who might not seek it, and their performance may suffer.

Span of control

Figure 17: A chain of command

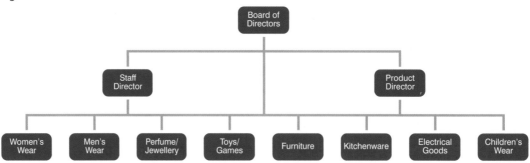

In some firms the chain of command is product based, for example, a department store where the manager of each department has a degree of responsibility.

A **chain of command** indicates the lines of authority and responsibility within a business. It may be long or short.

A **hierarchy** describes the layers of management in an organisation. Each layer has authority over the one beneath. Organisations may be tall with many layers or flat with fewer layers.

Span of control refers to the number of people in an organisation for whom one person is responsible.

Empowerment involves giving subordinates power over their working lives. Employees have some influence on the way they carry out their tasks.

Figure 18 shows how a long chain of command and a narrow span of control might work. A business with a number of operations could be organised with a board of directors, then a managing director and a strategy director, with marketing and finance reporting to the md, and research & development/engineering and business direction reporting to the strategy director. Each of these would have north and south geographically based departments reporting to them. Beneath that would be divisional area departments. This type of management structure could work well for a company operating all over the country.

Figure 18: Long chains of command and narrow spans of control

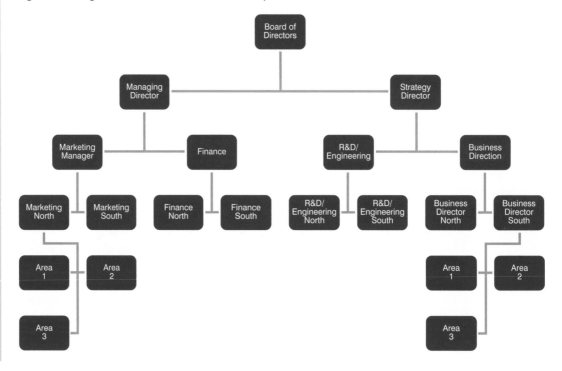

Whilst it could be argued that there are too many levels of command in Figure 18, the advantage of such a system is that quality control can be managed effectively. People who work together will get to know each other well and the system may foster good working relationships. Of course, decisions take longer to pass down this type of tall organisational structure.

Hierarchies

The Forestry Commission

The Forestry Commission cares for 827,000 hectares of sustainably managed woods and forests, and plants over 17,000 trees a year. It is a government department which employs over 3,000 people in Britain.

Many organisations are typically set up in a hierarchical structure. They may be structured by product, function or geography. Department stores, for example are structured by product, e.g. menswear, furniture, cosmetics. UK government departments are usually structured by function, e.g. Health or Education. The Forestry Commission is structured geographically, with a Board of Commissioners across Great Britain and national committees for Scotland, England and Wales.

Geographical structure allows decisions to be made and managed at a regional level. Decision-making is delegated down the hierarchy so that there is a measure of decentralisation. Each country manages its own estates and oversees conservation activities.

There are also benefits from centralisation, with some internal policy decisions made at the top of the hierarchy. This ensures consistency, for example, when implementing international rules for sustainable forestry management. Centralisation also provides the benefits of economies of scale, e.g. central departments for Human Resources, Finance and Information Services. Sharing services in this way reduces costs.

Some hierarchies have many layers and a narrow span of control with each manager being responsible for only a few workers. These tall organisations allow tighter control and supervision but may stifle workers' initiative. The Forestry Commission has a flat organisational structure with few layers and larger spans of control. Communication is generally quicker and enables creative approaches and the freedom to explore new options. Employees are able to take responsibility for their decisions.

Questions

1. What is meant by the term 'hierarchy'?

2. Organisations can be structured by product, function or geography. Explain each of these, using an example to illustrate your understanding.

3. Contrast the benefits received by the Forestry Commission from centralised decision making and decentralised decision making.

4. In your own words explain why the Forestry Commission benefits most from a flat organisational structure.

Businesses vary enormously. No single model of organisational structure is suitable for all businesses. In particular businesses need to decide between a flatter and a taller hierarchy. To create an effective organisational structure, a business needs to consider the following:

- The competition – research them, even if only by looking at published sources of information.

- The industry – is there a standard model? For example, the motor industry tends to work on a regional model.

- Regulation – certain aspects of the law may require a firm to set up in a particular way. This can range from payroll and taxation procedures to parliamentary law, for example, in the pharmaceutical industry.

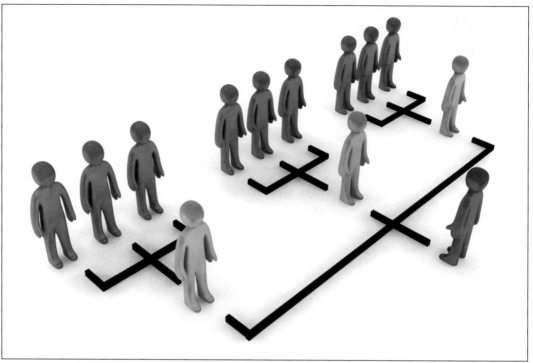

A clear organisation structure will show who is responsible to whom.

- Goals – the organisational structure should enable a firm to achieve its goals; a clear structure will outline how each person or each role will be undertaken, for example who is responsible to whom.

- Investors – firms need to create a favourable impression to potential investors. Alongside business plans, budgets and forecasts a clear organisational structure will help show how a firm hopes to achieve its objectives.

Find out more

In recent years schools and colleges have adapted their organisational structures, which have traditionally been fairly flat. There are many tasks and roles that were previously carried out by teaching staff; this model has now changed. Some of these tasks and roles are now being carried out by non-teaching staff, mainly administrative staff. Find out what has changed in your establishment, why it has changed, and whether it has changed for the better.

Present a short group report to your class and discuss your findings.

Recruitment and training

Redundancies

It might seem odd to start with redundancies when thinking about recruitment. In fact, the difficulties involved in recruiting people with scarce skills make it very important to retain employees who already have them. But redundancies are important for other reasons too: when they are a real problem in the economy, it will be much easier for employers to find the kind of people they want.

On September 2011, the UK government announced job losses of 80,000 in the three months to July, a rising trend. The jobless total at that point stood at 2.51 million or 7.9 per cent. Youth unemployment rose in the same period by 78,000 to 973,000.

Recession

The government's commitment to cutting back the public sector and reducing public borrowing made job losses inevitable. During 2011 pay rose by 2.8 per cent (2.1 per cent if bonuses were stripped out) while inflation was above 5% so real wages fell. Interest rates were low.

There are consequences for firms seeking to recruit. As the supply of labour goes up, relative to demand, then prices (wage rates) fall. There was a rise in the minimum wage in October 2011, (up from £5.93 per hour to £6.08 per hour for employees aged 21 and over with corresponding rises for younger workers). But there was little pressure on wage rates. Employers were able to get good quality staff for any vacancy for less than would be the case in times of relatively full employment.

In those conditions, people seeking work may need a higher level of skills and qualifications even at lower rates of pay. It is a buyers market. Employers will be looking for various skills from potential employees and, because of the number of potential applicants for each post, will be more likely to get them. Those seeking work will have to be even better prepared, show greater ingenuity and a positive attitude if they are to be successful. A downside for employers is the likely increased cost of sifting through hundreds of applications.

1. What is meant by the phrase 'a buyers market' in the context of the labour market?

2. Why might some employers be looking for employees with few formal skills or qualifications?

3. In periods of relatively full employment, employers try to keep key workers even when they are not fully occupied. Why might they do this?

Recruitment

Is there a vacancy?

The process of recruitment should start with an assessment of whether there really is a vacancy to be filled. When someone leaves, it is not always the case that the post needs filling. If roles can be changed and working practices can be altered, the business may not need a new recruit. A job analysis should be carried out – a process of describing and recording aspects of a job, and specifying the skills needed to do it. This will help to show whether the work can be reorganised and continue without recruiting.

Businesses often find themselves planning a smaller workforce. They may want to introduce new labour-saving technologies, or just see a way to produce more efficiently. The preferred way to deal with this is natural wastage – simply not replacing the departing employee. It avoids the many miseries associated with redundancies.

Internal or external candidates?

Sometimes **internal recruitment** is possible. If there is an employee who is appropriate for the job in question, the employer is spared the expense of advertising and processing applications. The candidate's knowledge of the business will be useful too. But before that decision can be made, everyone concerned must be aware of the law on fairness.

Employment law states that:

> "An employer has the legal responsibility to ensure that no unlawful discrimination occurs in the recruitment and selection process on the grounds of sex, race, disability, age, sexual orientation, and religion or belief. Equality of opportunity is an integral part of the recruitment and selection process."
>
> Source: ACAS

Employers should not promote someone from within an organisation without going through an application and interview process. If they do, there may be a complaint from another employee to an organisation such as the Advisory, Conciliatory and Arbitration Service (ACAS). This is likely to be costly for the firm concerned; it may create bad publicity, and may put off potential future employees from applying. In practice the appointment of staff from within, without formal procedures, still goes on in some firms and industries, particularly when there may be many applicants for a widely advertised job.

External recruitment

Larger firms are more likely to recruit externally, even though they probably have a bigger pool of possible internal applicants, who could be given the opportunity to apply. External recruitment, especially for larger firms, is more likely to attract a higher calibre of candidate, particularly when the post that needs filling is a challenging one.

Internal recruitment means that the employer looks for potential applicants within the organisation.

External recruitment means advertising a job vacancy widely enough to attract good applications from outside the organisation.

There are a number of Acts of Parliament that deal with discrimination. Whether they are recruiting internally or externally, employers must be aware of these. Of course, an employer can look to recruit externally but end up selecting an internal applicant.

Some organisations have rules regarding when a post will be advertised internally or when it is to be advertised both internally and externally. Such decisions will normally depend on the seniority of the post; the more complex the job and the higher the skill level required, the more likely it will be that the job is advertised to external as well as internal applicants.

The recruitment process

It is important that firms have good recruitment and selection procedures. If the process ends with a poor appointment for the organisation, the employer could be faced with increased **labour turnover** and increased costs. Also, the morale of other workers may fall if they have to cover for an inefficient colleague or don't enjoy their work because of a poor atmosphere.

> **Labour turnover** refers to the number of employees leaving the business each year, as a percentage of the average labour force.

Recruitment systems should be:

- Efficient – cost effective in terms of methods and resources.
- Effective – produce enough suitable candidates to ensure the identification of the one best fitted for the job.
- Fair – ensuring that right through the process, decisions are made on merit alone.

Job analysis

The job analysis will focus on the nature of the work and the skills required. A **job description** should then follow – a set of tasks, functions and responsibilities that make up a role; this may also include the qualifications needed to fill the post. Finally a **person specification** is required – a profile of the type of person needed to do the job. Often person specifications include the education and qualification required of the applicant, their training and experience and the personal qualities that would be appropriate. These characteristics may be split into two categories, essential and desired.

> **Job descriptions** set out all aspects of the work involved, define the responsibilities of the employee and show how they would fit into the organisational structure of the business.
>
> **Person specifications** describe the personal qualities that the applicant will need to be successful in the job.

Show what you know

1. Why do some firms make appointments from existing staff, without considering external advertising?

2. Is it more or less advantageous for a firm to appoint after an external recruitment process rather than an internal one? *(I hope your answer starts with 'it depends'.)*

3. If an external candidate is appointed to a post, when there are internal candidates, what extra qualities might that candidate bring to the post, and what problems might (s)he be faced with?

Increasingly, human resource management (HRM) departments are using recently developed software to digitise their employee information systems. This integrates payroll systems with workforce management information and makes it much easier for managers to use each individual member of the workforce in the most productive way. If in a large business an employee becomes redundant in one department, the information about them can be used to redeploy them to another department where their skills and personal qualities will still be of value.

Skills

Attitude or skills?

In small firms the use of press advertising and Jobcentres is often omitted in favour of word-of-mouth. The advantages of lower costs are obvious, and hiring someone who is a 'known quantity' can sometimes reduce staff turnover if the new member gets on well with the other staff. In small firms working relationships tend to be closer and more personal, and attitudes can be especially important. But there can also be indirect discrimination against disadvantaged groups.

Recruitment by word-of-mouth may help recruit people with a positive attitude but not necessarily those with the highest skills. In small firms wages may be lower and training less frequent. There are low levels of unionisation and less job security and it is these firms that are most likely to use word-of-mouth recruitment. But it may be hard to find the best possible recruits without advertising externally, widening the pool from which the employer is selecting.

Training

Who's best?

Ron Jepson ran his own handyman business. He was a jack-of-all-trades; he hoped he was a master of some of them as well. His order book was full and with the help of the local college he was able to take on an assistant, for a kind of apprenticeship. There was no agreement that a job would be available at the end of the year's course but it became clear to Ron that the only way he could progress further was to take on a full time employee.

Mike Dobson was the apprentice. Ron's wife said that she had never met a young man so polite and attentive. His timekeeping was good and he learnt quickly. Ron was not so sure. Mike had a habit of taking odd days off work, usually on Mondays, which made Ron doubt Mike's commitment. He was also very quiet, not even discussing the weekend's sport.

Ron wondered whether he should advertise the post, knowing that Mike might not be too pleased, or stick with Mike as he had already been trained.

Advise Ron, identifying the advantages and disadvantages of each approach and drawing a conclusion.

Some organisations want their recruits to have very specific skills and experience. This will mean that little time and money needs to be spent on training. Other organisations look for the kind of person who has a good attitude to work and to colleagues, and will fit well into a team. The argument for this approach is that recruits can always be trained in the necessary skills, but attitudes are hard to change.

How much training

Appropriate training will enhance the quality of the staff and their output, whether it is administrative, manual or technology based. Well trained staff may well seek to further their progress elsewhere but that is no reason not to train them. A firm that does not keep its employees aware of the latest and best advancements in the workplace will ultimately lose orders and profit.

Training can make employees feel valued as well as giving them a specific skill. They are likely to be better motivated if they feel the firm is looking after them. Some staff may need to be persuaded about training if they are comfortable with their situation and don't like change. Managers should be sympathetic but should still insist that they are up-to-date with the latest techniques.

Training can take many forms

- **Induction training** helps new recruits to settle quickly into the organisation by making sure that they know as much as possible about the work, the company policies and their terms and conditions of employment.

- **On-the-job training** allows the business to concentrate on the skills that they most need. It works well when the skills required are particular to that organisation. It is often appropriate in the service sector and can range from 'how to deal with customers' to the provision of I.T. training for administrative posts. This type of training may initially hinder the speed of work of those who carry out the training but at the same time good working relationships may be forged.

- **Off-the-job training** is carried out externally. Although there are fewer apprenticeships than in the past, many firms prefer to train off the job. Sometimes employees spend one or two days a week at college acquiring specific qualities and qualifications. This is probably best suited to younger employees, as they are cheaper to employ and government sponsored training schemes will reduce the cost of training to the employer. This approach works well in the manufacturing and construction sectors. The type of training arranged will depend on the type and size of the organisation.

Firms who value their staff and treat them well will be the long-term beneficiaries in terms of efficient, well trained staff who enjoy their work and working environment. Well motivated staff will keep staff turnover down.

> *Show what you know*
>
> 1. What is the difference between on-the-job training and off-the-job training?
>
> 2. If training is costly is it worth spending thousands of pounds on specialist courses for staff?
>
> 3. What is the link between well motivated staff and low labour turnover?

Labour turnover

Labour turnover

Labour turnover measures the rate at which employees leave their jobs.

$$\text{Labour turnover} = \frac{\text{Number leaving per year}}{\text{Average number of employees}} \times 100$$

Consider the following statement:

"A single event of recruitment is likely to have more effect on a small firm than on a large one."

Appointing a new person inappropriately in a business that has 15 employees is likely to impact on every employee. In a business that employs 1500 people the ripples are less likely to be felt. All appointments should go through a rigorous procedure, so as to avoid poor appointments, which may in the end lead to increased labour turnover.

Many businesses carry out regular appraisals of their employees, perhaps setting targets and discussing ways of working. Before starting on a round of appraisals, the business should know the percentage of labour turnover. A low labour turnover rate, reflecting the ability to retain staff, is an indication that the firm is doing something right. Employees are more likely to be happy in their work, less likely to take unwarranted time off and more likely to help increase the effectiveness of the organisation. If labour turnover is high, appraisals can be used as an opportunity to uncover possible causes and remedies.

High labour turnover is costly because new employees have to be recruited and this usually requires some training. Low labour turnover will be a significant advantage in maintaining competitiveness.

Chapter 19 **Motivation**

Life at Google

Google's approach to motivation is quite unusual. At their headquarters in California free food, pool tables and massages are available to employees. They are encouraged to spend 20% of their time working on projects that interest them. Recreational facilities are spread about the 'Googleplex' as it is called. Employees are encouraged to sit around on the bean bags discussing their work and thinking up innovative ideas. The company was formed in 1999; it has grown spectacularly and is perhaps the most successful in its field.

Google says its company culture is built around 'mission, innovation, fun and reward'. Quotes from the company include "you can make money without doing evil," "you can be serious without a suit," and "work should be challenging and the challenge should be fun."

The Google way to reward employees is to target small teams that are performing exceptionally well. The company aims to deliver rewards just at the right time, i.e. immediately they have achieved a goal. Sometimes the reward will be free company shares.

Questions

1. Why do you think the Google strategy works? Think of three reasons.

2. What is it about the company that makes this philosophy successful?

3. Would other companies ever be able to make it work?

A number of studies have been carried out to discover why people work. Besides money, there are many reasons why people go to work. Many people have worked to put money in their pockets and meals on the table but they have also established firm friendships. Many men had hard working lives because conditions at work in the past were often not good but they looked forward to seeing their mates. They enjoyed the sense of belonging to a group, and to a company.

Maslow

Abraham Maslow was the first to examine the needs of people at work and to find out what might motivate them. Maslow placed these needs in a hierarchy:

- Physiological needs, such as the basics of food, drink and good working conditions.

- Safety needs, such as job security and safe working conditions.

- Social needs, such as a sense of belonging and being loved, working with colleagues who provide support for you in a group situation.

- Esteem needs, such as being given recognition for doing a job well.

- Self-actualisation, such as being promoted or being given more responsibility in order to achieve full potential.

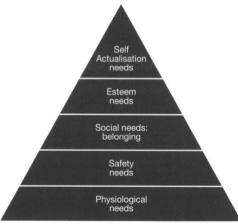

Figure 19: Maslow's hierarchy of needs

Maslow's hierarchy of needs identified the needs that relate to obtaining basic requirements to sustain life, as well as the higher order psychological needs that can make work satisfying.

The hierarchy of needs

Maslow argued that the needs on the bottom rung of the pyramid or hierarchy had to be satisfied before a person could move to the next level. This means that before an employee can be 'productive' at work the employer must pay the employee enough money to enable him or her to survive (the **physiological needs**). The employer will also need to provide for the **safety needs** before the employee can maximise potential.

Each level of needs is dependent on the one before. Critics of the theory argue that is very difficult to say when a particular level has been achieved. How, for instance, are **social needs** for friendliness, love and belonging to be achieved if employees don't work together? Some employees work from home, or are out on customer calls; their only contact with the firm is an electronic one.

Esteem needs are achieved by gaining the respect of others and gaining recognition. This can be met by praise or a monetary reward but is it necessary to have achieved, for example, love and belonging, the social needs, first? **Self actualisation** – the need for a person to fulfil their potential, is a worthy aim but for some people, this may never be achieved.

People in the workplace are motivated by many different things and it would be wrong to suggest that if a person does not fulfil their potential they cannot be motivated. Maslow's work was detailed – much more than just the diagram in Figure 19. The theory should not be cast aside because not everyone quite fits the model. Businesses do value and make use of Maslow's theory. If managers can identify where an employee is on the hierarchy, they have a starting point for deciding on the reward that is needed.

F.W. Taylor

Taylor's scientific management

Maslow, writing in the 1950s, was the first to look at employees' needs, and how they related to each other. But he was not the first to consider motivation. It is 100 years since Frederick W. Taylor carried out research on the factors that motivate individuals. Taylor still has many followers.

Taylor's research was carried out in a steelworks in the USA. He was a well educated man, who spent some time working on the factory shop floor, gaining rapid promotion. He was well placed to see that the work routine at the time was haphazard; that workers often brought their own tools into work and made their own decisions as to how a job should be done.

Taylor sought to improve industrial efficiency by studying each task carefully and training workers to carry them out according to scientific principles. He believed that workers left to their own devices would do as little as possible. He proposed a clear demarcation line between management and workers, which had not previously existed. Workers were to be rewarded by having pay linked to productivity.

> **Scientific management** as set out by F.W. Taylor called for work-study analysis of each job, to determine the most efficient ways of producing. He based his organisation of the work place on the scientific data and created an incentive by linking pay to the level of output.

Successful but controversial

Taylor's ideas were forerunners of what in the mid-20th century came to be known as time and motion: each worker was observed and each element of work was timed. His methods were hugely successful but much criticised in some quarters; some people felt that workers were being treated like machines. His way of working didn't allow for differences in human performance. This, according to critics, dehumanised the person carrying out the job.

Many of Taylor's ideas were followed slavishly and successfully for three-quarters of a century. His initial observations were carried out at the Bethlehem Steel works in the USA. His methods were responsible for raising pig-iron production by almost 400 per cent per day, yet his approach of 'one best way' to do the job was not popular among employees, despite their benefiting from higher pay if they did well. Many factory owners were critical and did not use his methods.

The American singer Billy Joel, writing in the 1980s in a song called Allentown, included the lines 'our graduations hang on the wall, they never really helped us at all, they never told us what was real, iron and coke, chromium steel'. And so it was in the USA, at least until the the steel works closed down. Taylor gave them 75 good years.

Show what you know

1. Outline the advantages and disadvantages to using Maslow's Hierarchy of Needs as a means of motivating a workforce.

2. F.W. Taylor believed that the main motivational force in the workplace was the financial reward for being productive. What benefits does this bring to (a) the employer and (b) the employee?

3. In your opinion is Taylor's Scientific Management approach to work and motivation the right one? Explain.

Motivation Factors

Herzberg

A crude summary of Taylor's work would suggest that financial incentives motivate workers and some would say that is true today. Other studies suggest that there is more to motivation than just monetary reward. Frederick Herzberg, a psychologist, began studying motivation shortly after the end of World War II. From observations he made after studying a group of professional engineers and accountants he developed the two-factor Motivation-Hygiene Theory of job satisfaction. Herzberg's findings led him to believe that the following Motivation Factors gave people job satisfaction:

- Achievement
- Recognition
- Work itself
- Responsibility
- Promotion
- Growth

Hygiene Factors

Herzberg argued that workers would be more productive if these factors were in place. But equally important were the Hygiene Factors, which needed to be in place to prevent workers from becoming dissatisfied. The Hygiene factors were not Motivators, but they did matter.

- Company policy and administration
- Supervision
- Working conditions
- Pay and benefits
- Relationships with co-workers
- Personal life
- Status
- Job security

It is important to highlight that according to Herzberg, an improvement in hygiene factors is not likely to motivate an individual but if they are not met or if there is some deterioration in them, there will be a fall in productivity.

Herzberg identified and distinguished between the Hygiene and Motivation needs of employees. He showed how hygiene needs would avoid dissatisfaction while motivation needs would actually contribute to job satisfaction.

Herzberg's research

Figure 20: Satisfaction and dissatisfaction

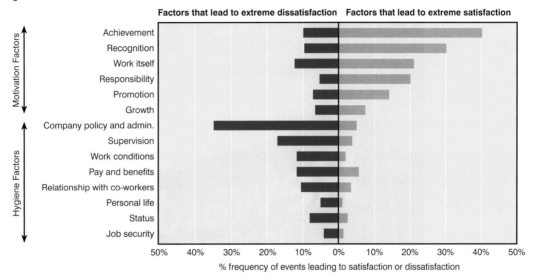

Herzberg's theory aligns more closely with Maslow than with Taylor. Improving pay and conditions should remove some dissatisfaction but will that be enough? If in a year's time, for instance, a higher pay claim is made and refused then presumably the dissatisfaction returns. Herzberg's study was on a small group of workers with specific skills. Follow up studies on different groups of workers have failed to replicate Herzberg's findings. What has stood the test of time is the link between Herzberg's work and that of empowerment which is covered in Chapter 20.

Motivating staff at The Body Shop

The late Anita Roddick was famous for her ideas on how to motivate her staff. She said:

- All staff should ask questions and look for better ways of working.
- Listen to new ideas – they keep everyone interested and help them to innovate.
- Respond to suggestions.
- If profits are growing, share them with the staff.
- Make heroes of the staff who perform well.
- Be family friendly.
- Ask staff "how can we ennoble your life?" and "how can we make your spirit sing?".
- Allow staff to grow.

Her overall motivational philosophy was 'staff are motivated by being given the opportunity to have ownership of the goals and values of the company'.

Anita Roddick withdrew from involvement with The Body Shop before she died, but her ideas on motivation were influential. Some of them were quirky and probably wouldn't suit everyone, but they were in use when the company was growing at its fastest.

Questions

1. What connections are there between Anita Roddick's approach and the motivation theories? Find at least three and explain each one.

2. How might Anita Roddick's ideas work in (a) a construction company, (b) an airline and (c) a supermarket?

3. To what extent is money a motivating force?

4. According to Herzberg, pay and benefits do not motivate workers but recognition and achievement do. Outline the thinking behind this view and consider its relevance to today's workforce.

Firms need to set out quite clearly how they will reward their employees.

Special tip

Don't just learn the theories. Make sure you can apply them in practical contexts. Don't forget about McGregor's Theory X and Theory Y in Unit 1. Show how Taylor, Herzberg and Maslow's ideas work in practice, using lots of examples and practical applications. These are all the theories you need to know for the Edexcel course; the examiners are always interested when work from other theorists is mentioned, but no questions will be set on their work.

Pay as a motivator

Financial incentives

I bought my first car from an old friend. I remember him saying "one down, seventeen to go". He had to sell 9 new cars and 18 used cars in order to qualify for a bonus. This would be on top of the commission he got from each sale. It was a very tough target; he never made it but he said that no one ever did. To me that was demoralising, but to him it was something to aim for. As long as he was ahead of his fellow salesmen he didn't mind. So no bonus was awarded.

> A **bonus** is a one off payment in recognition of the contribution made to the firm – in the case above, selling a certain number of cars.
>
> **Commission** is a payment of a percentage of the value of each product or service sold.

Pay is important to people; it is also important to employers as it is often the biggest single cost to a firm, regularly accounting for more than 50 per cent of total costs in some businesses. Pay can also be a source of unrest if employees feel they are being treated unfairly.

Firms need to set out quite clearly how they will reward their employees. They need to be transparent if they want to avoid a lot of unrest and dissatisfaction. This doesn't mean to say everyone will agree with every decision but at least staff will know the basis of that decision. Often people are paid a basic wage and may qualify for 'extras' depending on the type of work. Employees need to believe that they are being rewarded fairly.

The minimum wage

The minimum wage in the UK at the end of 2011 was £6.08 an hour for employees aged 21 and over. Many hundreds of thousands of workers are paid minimum wage, from shop workers to care home assistants, from farm workers to hairdressers. The increase in 2011 was 15p. For a 40 hour shift that is an extra £6 per week, not a lot for the individual, but some firms said it would lead to job losses. However, some said this in 1999 when the minimum wage was introduced. This minimum rate is a payment for the amount of time employees spend at work, i.e. a time rate. It provides little in the way of an incentive.

Paying employees an overtime rate for work done over and above the standard time may be an incentive. Many factories would pay their operatives time-and-a–half for working on a Saturday morning and double time for working on a Sunday. Part-time work and split shifts are now more common so there are fewer incentivised rates for overtime.

A good rate of pay attracts reliable employees and often works as a rationing device. If the initial rate is high some people will not apply for vacant posts as they realise they don't have what is required. Others will chance it if clear indications of the necessary experience and qualifications are not set out.

You can take a horse to water...

George Thompson owned a number of newsagents and over a period of 25 years was successful. For a man with little formal education he did remarkably well. He used to believe that his employees needed to be persuaded to work hard by some form of stimulus and that without it they wouldn't work as hard.

George had an employee of the month award, voted for by his customers; he would encourage competition amongst his paper boys and girls by rewarding the ones who delivered their papers within a set period of time and without any complaints from householders. The rewards were simple and probably sounded a bit silly, to adults. A free ice cream to the first paper boy back, and an extra day's pay if there were no complaints in a month, were typical rewards. He even got his staff to believe that not deducting money from their pay when the till didn't balance was a reward.

George rewarded staff for loyalty and was always generous at Christmas. He used to praise highly and had high expectations of his staff. Few let him down. He treated customers well and his staff better. He was fair and would always check on staff when they were ill. He had a uniform for his staff which he paid for and he set staff work-related targets – he used to call them his 'goal of the month'. (He thought this was very funny.) George was often surprised at how successful he was. Perhaps you wouldn't be!

Questions

1. George had never heard of any motivational theory or theorist. Of the motivational theories you have learnt, which one(s) fit most closely to George's philosophy? Explain your answer.

2. In what way would you reward staff who are loyal to you?

3. What do you think were the main reasons for George's success in business?

Profit related pay

Performance related pay

A good initial rate of pay may be part of a remuneration package that might also include **profit sharing**. Profit sharing encourages employees or partners in a business to be as productive as possible as they will (usually) get a predetermined, equal percentage share of the profit. Similarly employees may get a bonus related to the profits made; usually a proportion of the profits are set aside for this use. This is known as **profit related pay**.

At John Lewis all the profit remaining after investment is ploughed back into the business is shared amongst the employees. This percentage has been as high as 15 per cent of earnings. The main problem with these last two types of financial incentive is that they are paid to everyone regardless of their level of performance.

This can prove frustrating for hard-working employees who see less hard working employees getting the same reward.

A similar sounding concept which is actually quite different from profit sharing and profit related pay is **performance related pay**. Here workers are judged and rewarded individually, according to how they have performed. This incentive has become more popular in some industries where there has been a move away from industry-wide agreements to local agreements, allowing for a greater focus on individual and team performances.

Profit sharing gives employees a percentage of profits as well as basic pay.

Profit related pay relates a proportion of pay directly to the level of profit. In the UK there is a tax incentive to pay this way, but it has not been widely adopted.

Performance related pay usually consists of a bonus related to employee achievement of some kind. The targets against which performance is measured could for example be related to output or quality or customer service.

Employees are usually subject to an appraisal or a review or assessment each year where their performance is measured against some known, pre-established criteria. Depending on particular schemes, a successful employee may move up the pay scale or receive a small cash payment or bonus. Anyone who does not match up to expectations receives only the basic wage or salary. There is a presumption that employees will be motivated by this type of performance related pay. However there is a danger that some awards may appear to be subjective if targets are unclear. Sometimes employees come to expect a reward of some sort regardless of their performance. (This seems to apply in banking.)

In the past, it was common for employees to be paid **piece-rates**, which meant paying according to how many items had been produced. Taylor saw this as the best way to motivate workers. This approach is now little used even in manufacturing situations. However many people still get a commission payment if they make a sale.

Piece-rates had their attractions for hard working employees, as long as there was a plentiful supply of work to be done, i.e. there were enough pieces to make. The method didn't work very well if there was a bottleneck in production or if there were problems with delivery and rigorous quality control procedures were required.

Piece-rates are wages paid according to the amount produced. Fruit pickers are sometimes paid this way.

Show what you know

1. Explain 'commission' and give an example of its use.

2. Why might some employees view profit sharing and profit related pay as unfair?

3. What are the essential features of a good pay scheme?

4. What is a piece-rate system and what problems might there be for employees on such a system?

5. Why is performance related pay easier to establish at local rather than a national level?

Chapter 20

How managers can get the best from their staff

Why not delegate?

We are sorry if you are inconvenienced but we will be closed for the next fortnight as we are on holiday/our daughter is getting married/there has been a bereavement in the family.

How often do you see a notice like the one above? Each set of circumstances is a valid reason for disruption but is it enough to lose two weeks' business, especially if there are other, perhaps junior, members of staff available to help? What better way could there be of getting the best from your staff than giving them responsibility and empowerment? To know that you are trusted to deal with customers and suppliers, to pay money into the bank and to keep records, could be rewarding for an employee.

Question

Of course not everyone is able to get that opportunity but what does it say about the quality of staff if an employer is unwilling to make that decision?

Delegation means passing authority down from a superior to a subordinate (from boss to employee). It gives a boost to the confidence of the subordinates. It makes them feel valued. It can be carried out at different levels. Delegation is a step on the way to empowerment, where an employee is allowed to take control of some decision making. If an employee is given delegated authority only when 'the boss' is busy, or feels overworked, they may feel resentful.

Delegation is probably easier when the superior works closely with the subordinate as they should each know the other's capabilities. Even here there are rules to follow. Planning is a key element; delegation should not be attempted unless there is complete clarity about what is being delegated, otherwise confusion will reign. Tasks should be discussed and, where appropriate, explanations provided.

When an employee is given authority and responsibility to implement a decision, there is some degree of empowerment. Employees who have been empowered have some control over how they achieve their work objectives. They work autonomously without management direction.

> **Delegation** means passing responsibility on to someone lower down the hierarchy, so that decisions are, as far as possible, taken by those who have to implement them.

Communication

Consultation

The business climate is often challenging; recession or an increasingly competitive market can mean that orders and profits are hard to come by. Businesses that have performed well in the past are quite likely to do so in the future but sometimes they have to make important decisions that affect staff morale. Remuneration is always a contentious area and decisions to cut back on staff, to reduce the working week and to cut wages, are never welcome.

Consulting the workforce usually helps and is never a bad thing. Not consulting the workforce is rarely a good idea. Employees who find that they are going on a 3 day week, for example, want that decision to be explained to them. They might not like it but they might see that it is the best decision in the circumstances if there is a rationale behind it. Employers who go out of their way to keep staff informed, to have consultation sessions and to report back to their staff, are more likely to get their backing than those managers who issue instructions from on high.

Not consulting

In 2003, The Accident Group, a personal injury claims management company, became insolvent and went into administration (in common speech, it went bust). It told its 2,400 employees that they would all be made redundant by text message. The staff were so disgusted that they took away all the computer equipment when they left.

Question

Imagine that you are going to be asked to work a 3-day week for the next 4 months. Explain your reaction, (a) if you are consulted and (b) if you are not.

Organising production

Team work

The phrase 'throw a spanner in the works' means, literally, damaging a motor engine or gearbox by putting a foreign object into the moving parts. This could be a way of describing the disruption of production lines in car factories. The phrase is used to mean ruining a plan or deliberately causing trouble.

Long established vehicle manufacturing plants with big assembly lines have had a history of disruption and disagreement with trade unions. Assembly lines made for big increases in productivity when they were developed in the mid 20th century. But they resulted in many employees having just one or two tasks, which were repeated over and over again. When Japanese cars began to sell well in the West, they were generally found to be more reliable than the home-produced competing cars. The entire motor vehicle industry started to rethink. In time manufacturers of all kinds of products were influenced by what followed.

Renault

At Renault in the 1970s there was a record of spectacular conflicts, growing absenteeism and a high level of labour turnover, along with an increase in product faults that had to be rectified. This led to a form of team work. Initially assembly line workers would rotate between 2 or 3 positions. This was followed by giving small groups of workers control of the complete assembly of a mechanism, e.g. the gearbox, whilst it moved down the line. Sometimes this included preparation and rectification procedures.

Not everyone at Renault was happy with this. The Work Study department felt that it went against the principle of having each employee specialise in one operation. In time, the company adapted new technologies, automating some processes whilst having small groups of employees standing by to intervene when problems arose. (Robots were gradually being introduced at this time.)

Similar trends gradually appeared in most of the Western vehicle manufacturers' plants. Often, teams were made responsible for maintaining quality assurance.

Questions

1. Why did production systems where each employee specialised in one task cause problems?

2. Explain why teamwork has been associated with a trend towards higher quality and reliability in consumer products.

The principal function of **team work** is to improve the quality of work whilst increasing productivity, by being better organised and getting together to solve problems. This was made possible by having fewer operatives on the assembly line and fewer replacement operatives. Quality control and replacement of defective parts, as well as cleaning, were kept within the group. Workers would become skilled in a wider range of tasks and would develop greater pride in their work; there would be fewer disagreements. This has worked well for many businesses but introducing new ways of working entails very careful planning and willingness to accept change. This kind of reorganisation cannot be adopted lightly.

Flexible working

There are two aspects to **flexible working**:

- Being prepared to take on a range of different tasks within the production process.

- Accepting a range of employment patterns, including part-time as well as full-time, temporary as well as permanent jobs, and varying the hours worked to suit the situation.

Multiskilling

In a flexible workforce, many employees will be **multiskilled**. They will be able to carry out a number of different processes. They may have a good understanding of the equipment they work with and be able to do minor repairs when needed. They will probably have had some recent training to help them get used to new technologies. They are likely to be familiar with lean production methods.

This approach will fit neatly with delegation, empowerment, team work and quality assurance. For many businesses, it has helped to increase productivity because it encourages employees to adapt readily to changing circumstances. It may also be associated with a decentralised approach.

Some businesses want to move from a taller to a flatter hierarchy, which means **delayering**. In other words, a whole layer will be removed from the hierarchy, usually people who might be seen as middle managers. This will often require a degree of flexibility and some multiskilling, as responsibilities are redistributed amongst the workforce.

> **Flexible working** can mean being prepared to take on a number of different tasks, and also, being able and willing to work irregular hours, part time or temporarily.
>
> **Multiskilling** involves employees in being trained to undertake a range of different processes.
>
> **Delayering** means moving to a flatter management structure by removing a layer from the hierarchy.

Buoyant Upholstery

Mike Aramayo had been Managing Director of Buoyant Upholstery for five years, during which time he had eliminated losses and moved the company into profit. Sales and profits had increased but margins were very tight and competition was fierce. A series of meetings at Board level led him to believe that he needed to cut costs further.

Buoyant already had a flexible workforce, bringing temporary overseas workers into the UK at busy times of the year, and Mike didn't think there was much room for increased efficiency in the production area. The company had seven directors, all but one of them with over 20 years experience in the furniture business; each director had his or her own team. Mike wanted to delayer but instead of removing a complete level across the firm he decided to amalgamate four areas into two, combining the sales department with the commercial department, and the design department with the development department.

Two of the directors were made redundant (one was happy to go; after 35 years service he got a bumper payout) but the other director was not so happy. Ten other management and administration posts went as well. Cost savings were apparent immediately but the training budget increased as teams were amalgamated. Some employees' responsibilities increased and many became more empowered.

The new design team were quick to adapt with staff relishing the chance to make important decisions and to see them through. The new marketing and sales department found the flatter structure more challenging. However, one of the senior managers found it difficult to take responsibility for an increased number of employees. Instead of decisions being made more swiftly, there were areas of confusion and some communication problems in that department.

On reviewing the changes Mike became aware that not all employees reacted similarly to increased responsibility, despite an increase in the remuneration package. He appreciated the personal impact the changes were having on individuals and made a mental note to offer more support.

(questions overleaf)

Questions

1. What are the main reasons why firms choose to delayer?

2. At Buoyant Upholstery the removal of part of the management structure led to greater empowerment for some managers. What does empowerment mean in this context?

3. Why might a flatter structure lead to more, not fewer communication problems?

4. Suggest reasons why the changes appeared to have worked in one of the amalgamated areas but not the other.

Flexible working hours

Flexible employment patterns

Some businesses operate a policy of flexible working in terms of hours worked, days worked, split shifts and even working from home. These can benefit certain groups of workers – especially those who need working hours that are family-friendly. Part-time work is becoming much more common in the UK labour force, partly to accommodate the needs of families, but also to help businesses adapt to falling demand for their products. This trend has helped many businesses to cope with recession.

The proportion of woman in the workforce continues to increase and with it the need for greater flexibility. Many men and women appreciate flexible working hours. Students looking for part-time work are often open to changes in their work pattern and may prefer split shifts. Older workers may work for 3 days a week or on a mornings only basis. Many people have older family members to care for and try to fit their working hours around their needs.

There are a number of reasons why the traditional factory and office hours are no longer the norm, besides those already covered, for example:

- changes in technology require different approaches
- businesses facing stiff competition may look to cut costs by adopting a flexible approach.

Without doubt, the employer or manager who seeks to cater for the needs of staff and wants to be fair will get a better response from most employees. Employees who regard their working conditions as good are much more likely to work productively than those with grievances. Managers cannot resolve all problems but they can reduce the chance of working hours being one of them.

Non-financial incentives

Traditional assembly line work where each person specialised in one task led to many people doing seriously boring work. Other kinds of jobs can be boring too, and many of these are not well paid either. In order to keep morale up and costs down, different methods of working may be used. You will already be familiar with some of these – such as team work and quality circles, delegation and empowerment. Other developments have included:

- **Job rotation** allows employees to change tasks from time to time. They will move from one job to another, in a planned and organised way, getting any necessary training when they make the switch. This increases the range of their experience and can provide variety, new skills and enhanced motivation. This should reduce boredom although it may lead to a temporary fall in productivity while the worker learns a new skill. It fits in well with teamwork and makes employees more versatile.

- **Job enlargement** involves reorganising the various jobs to be done, giving each individual several different tasks, perhaps making them responsible for putting an entire product together. This enlarges the scope of the job and enhances the role of each employee in the production process. Job enlargement could be said to be a form of horizontal loading – more tasks of a similar nature. Employee satisfaction should rise.

- **Job enrichment** expands the process vertically. An employee might be given responsibility for planning, ordering materials, quality control, completing the job, and maintenance. This is more challenging and may not be suitable for everyone. It brings possibilities of recognition and achievement that may be a big motivating factor. This approach is not confined to manufacturing production; in fact it can be better suited to the administrative side of a business.

Job enhancement

Managers have to weigh up the relative effectiveness of these non-financial incentives, in order to make jobs more rewarding and get the best from their staff. No one type of job enhancement is going to improve matters for everyone. The nature of the job, the type of industry and the availability of workers will all need to be considered. The case study, Buoyant Upholstery, illustrates how flexibility can work in a wide range of ways, and the importance of fitting the changes to the needs of the people concerned.

Show what you know

1. To what extent might the measures discussed here contribute to meeting a) Maslow's higher order needs and b) Herzberg's motivation factors?

2. Why might job enhancement fit in well with making all employees responsible for quality, or a policy of continuous improvement?

Motivation again

A major research study tried to find out what motivated employees. It concluded that managers got the best from their employees by satisfying four basic motivating drives. These are:

● The drive to acquire (obtain scarce objects, including intangibles such as social status)

● The drive to bond (form connections with individuals and groups)

● The drive to comprehend (satisfy our curiosity and master the world around us)

● The drive to defend (protect against external threats and provide justice).

The study focused on four commonly used workforce indicators that measure motivation. These are: engagement, satisfaction, commitment and intention to quit. The study found that an organisation's ability to meet the four fundamental drives explains, on average, about 60 per cent of employees' variance on these four motivational indicators.

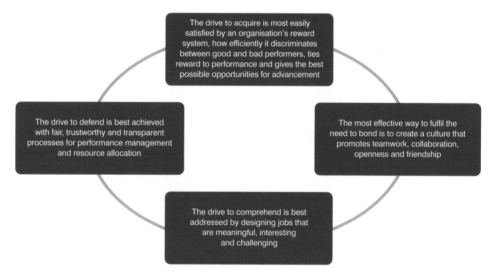

The drive to acquire is most easily satisfied by an organisation's reward system, how efficiently it discriminates between good and bad performers, ties reward to performance and gives the best possible opportunities for advancement

The drive to defend is best achieved with fair, trustworthy and transparent processes for performance management and resource allocation

The most effective way to fulfil the need to bond is to create a culture that promotes teamwork, collaboration, openness and friendship

The drive to comprehend is best addressed by designing jobs that are meaningful, interesting and challenging

Finally, workers felt that their immediate line manager had a big part to play in their motivational performance.

Questions

1. Which of the above 'drives' can best be satisfied by performance related pay?

2. Which one of the four drives could best be satisfied by team working?

3. Which one of the four drives could best be satisfied by job enrichment or job rotation?

4. In your opinion can any of the four drives be satisfied by empowerment?

The Nigel Clare Network Trust

The NCNT is a national UK charity that delivers practical support to families where a child's life is limited by quality, lifespan or both.

Recently The NCNT moved out of its Headquarters offices in London and adopted a flexible working structure based on working at home or at clients' sites. Despite the initial setup costs and ongoing support costs, there have been significant savings in annual operating costs.

The quality of client services actually improved as well and twenty per cent more families were supported. All staff now work at and from their homes but they meet on a regular basis for face-to-face team meetings, usually held in local business centres.

Source: Adapted from Wisework – making flexibility work

Questions

1. What are the benefits of flexible working for the NCNT?

2. Are there any disadvantages arising from NCNT's arrangements?

3. How has the advent of telecoms networking systems helped firms become more flexible?

Cutting costs

Some businesses can raise prices without losing demand. But many will find that they lose customers if they do try to increase the price. In a period of no growth or slow growth, it is unlikely that many industries will be able to raise prices without this having some effect on demand. In these situations firms will look to reduce costs, to help maintain their profit margins.

Economic history would tell us that the easiest way to do this is usually to reduce labour costs. This applies particularly to the service sector, where most businesses are labour intensive. But in manufacturing it may be possible to invest in equipment that requires fewer people to produce the necessary quantity of output. So either way, jobs are lost.

Flexible working

Making employees redundant is usually the last thing a firm or organisation considers. It can be costly in the short-run; it involves losing skilled workers and it can be politically sensitive. NCTN found a different way, by teleworking and hiring meeting rooms when they really needed to meet. This immediately removed the high cost of office space in London. This is one example of the way in which flexible working can cut costs.

Flexibility can be increased when employees work from home. Developments in computer technology make it less important for some workers to be at a central location. The ease of communication, through emails, social networking sites and video conference meetings such as skype, enables communication with people on the other side of the world. Some of the money spent on travel will be saved and the business doesn't have to provide permanent work stations for all employees.

There are several good ways to use a flexible workforce:

- by having split shifts – this works well for bars, takeaways and restaurants

- by bringing people in at short notice and paying them the same rate as everyone else. This is particularly useful for supermarkets

- by offering their workers short-term contracts. This helps to cut costs as they will have fewer statutory rights.

For example, a person on a contract for less than a year does not have any pension rights. Once the contract ends, the business has no need to re-employ that person. Often a contract is for only 3 month's duration and the cost implication for the firm ends at the end of that time.

Contracts and flexibility

Flexible contracts

Many firms will stipulate the number of hours an employee has to work but not the timing of those hours or even the number of days they have to be at work. This gives employees some flexibility when they need to make appointments or to make child care arrangements. However this system can also work against the employee. If the employer requires their presence when the business has a lot of work, this may be at a time that does not suit the employee.

For the business, flexible working can have many cost advantages:

- it may be able to employ first rate staff who would not otherwise be available

- having a contented workforce increases productivity and enables the business to cut its unit costs

- having people who can be called in whenever they are needed saves having to pay a full time employee who might not be fully occupied all the time

- it may be possible to retain able employees by creating working arrangements that suit them, when otherwise they might move elsewhere.

In law, employees who have worked for an employer for at least 26 weeks are entitled to ask for flexible working hours if they have responsibility for children under 17 or act as carers. The idea of flexi-time and of staggered hours should be of benefit to both firm and employee. It is worth re-iterating that if an employee believes the employer to acting in a caring and fair manner, the response from the worker will outweigh any inconvenience suffered by the business.

Sundays

Fifty years ago few business premises opened on a Sunday. Little sport was played. Times have changed! As society began to accept Sundays as a good day for leisure activities, so the need for more workers on the Sabbath became apparent. Employees were encouraged to work on a Sunday with the offer of higher wage rates. Then the law changed to make it easier for retail outlets to open on Sundays, creating increased demand for part-time workers and blurring the need to pay more for working anti-social hours. Probably, many of the people who now work at weekends don't consider their hours to be particularly anti-social.

Questions

1. List and explain at least four ways in which costs could be cut by flexible working.

2. Explain why retailers have generally welcomed the chance to open on Sundays.

Part-time working

There has been a shift in attitudes towards part-time working: 7.8 million people in the UK are either willing to work part-time or have to (figures for July 2011), out of a total workforce of 29 million. The biggest advantage for businesses is the cost saving: they can employ part timers at just the times when they most need them.

Not everyone likes part-time work and in 2011, 1 million people were working part time because they could not find full time work. At least, for them, part time work beats being unemployed.

For a business, part time employment facilitates many aspects of flexible working, in that it allows businesses to make use of people just when the need is greatest, and keeps overall employment costs down. Some

If a business is struggling some people may have to lose their jobs and be made redundant.

employers allow people with family commitments to work when they want to. Often this allows them to get a good recruit at a rate of pay that is less than the market wage for the job. It may please the employee as well.

Cutting the workforce

Staff dismissal and redundancy

Sometimes it becomes clear that particular employees are costing the business more to employ than they are actually contributing to output and sales revenue. This may not be the fault of the employee. The business may be struggling in a shrinking market, in which case the business may have to shrink too, just to stay alive. People who lose their jobs in this situation are being made redundant.

When an employee has actually made mistakes or failed to work in the way expected, the business will want to dismiss them. This is very different from redundancy.

● It may well be that this employee should never have been hired in the first place, because they were not the right person for the job.

● Or it may be that they had the right qualifications but they have not worked as expected.

Fair and unfair dismissal

When it becomes clear that the employee has significant shortcomings, managers must act in accordance with employment law. They must first give a verbal warning, making clear to the employee the ways in which they have been performing poorly and saying what they will have to do to keep the job. If this does not bring improvement, a second verbal warning is required, followed if necessary by a written warning. If the employer has followed these procedures and the employee can be shown to have performed badly, then dismissal is fair.

Sometimes an employee believes that the dismissal is unfair. Some people who are made redundant think this too. They may take their grievance to an industrial tribunal, which may find in their favour. This is expensive for the employer and usually, if the employee has a case, the business will seek to settle the dispute by paying some form of compensation before too many lawyers get involved.

Avoiding redundancies

Recently in the public sector there has been a wave of redundancies, including some in the armed forces and the caring professions. In the private sector, BAe Systems has announced job losses exceeding 3,000 at its plants in Lancashire and Yorkshire, amid howls of protest.

Redundancies cut costs in the long run. But most businesses want to avoid creating bad relationships with stakeholders and in particular, with the workforce and the local community. What are the alternatives? Most businesses will make every effort to reduce labour costs through all the forms of flexible working described above. They may also try various marketing tactics and new technologies. They may consider moving production abroad, which can cut costs dramatically but this is fraught with difficulties and unlikely to lessen the need for redundancies.

Voluntary labour turnover or compulsory redundancy?

If the conclusion is that redundancies are inevitable, the key component of a successful strategy will be discussion and communication. Managers must talk to trade unions or other representatives of the workforce. Together they may be able to find solutions that are acceptable.

- To some extent it may be possible to reduce the labour force by natural wastage, i.e. not replace employees who retire or leave for their own reasons.

- Maybe some staff would agree to voluntary redundancy, but some of these people may be quite valuable to the organisation, so it is never simple.

- Favourable redundancy payments may help reduce the numbers without any compulsory redundancies being needed.

- For further redundancies, a consensus may be found, whereby the outcome will be seen as fair and equitable. For example, a process of last in, first out may be used (i.e. making the most recent recruits redundant). This may not rid the firm of its least productive workers but it should help to avoid a poisonous atmosphere.

When there is a need to shed staff, the job must be done in a way that is seen as fair. It is also important to try to ensure that remaining employees do not become too fearful, starting to act like rats leaving a sinking ship. Here again, communication is important.

Index

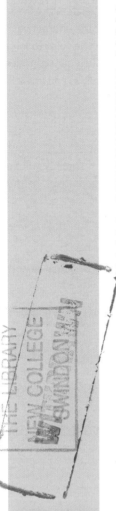